New

GW00992809

Edited by **Sally Welch**

January–April 2019

The Bible Reading Fellowship
15 The Chambers, Vineyard
Abingdon OX14 3FE
brf.org.uk

The Bible Reading Fellowship (BRF) is a Registered Charity (233280)

ISBN 978 0 85746 729 4
This edition © The Bible Reading Fellowship 2018

Cover image © Thinkstock; illustration, page 139: Assisi doorway © Molly Dowell

Distributed in Australia by:
MediaCom Education Inc, PO Box 610, Unley, SA 5061
Tel: 1 800 811 311 | admin@mediacom.org.au

Distributed in New Zealand by:
Scripture Union Wholesale, PO Box 760, Wellington
Tel: 04 385 0421 | suwholesale@clear.net.nz

Acknowledgements
Scripture quotations marked NRSV are taken from The New Revised Standard Version
of the Bible, Anglicised Edition, copyright © 1989, 1995 by the Division of Christian
Education of the National Council of the Churches of Christ in the USA. Used by
permission. All rights reserved.

NIV: The Holy Bible, New International Version, Anglicised edition, copyright © 1979,
1984, 2011 by Biblica. Used by permission of Hodder & Stoughton Publishers, an
Hachette UK company. All rights reserved. 'NIV' is a registered trademark of Biblica.
UK trademark number 1448790.

ESV: The Holy Bible, English Standard Version, published by HarperCollins Publishers,
© 2001 Crossway Bibles, a division of Good News Publishers. Used by permission.
All rights reserved.

Printed by Gutenberg Press, Tarxien, Malta

Suggestions for using *New Daylight*

Find a regular time and place, if possible, where you can read and pray undisturbed. Before you begin, take time to be still and perhaps use the BRF Prayer on page 6. Then read the Bible passage slowly (try reading it aloud if you find it over-familiar), followed by the comment. You can also use *New Daylight* for group study and discussion, if you prefer.

The prayer or point for reflection can be a starting point for your own meditation and prayer. Many people like to keep a journal to record their thoughts about a Bible passage and items for prayer. In *New Daylight* we also note the Sundays and some special festivals from the Church calendar, to keep in step with the Christian year.

New Daylight and the Bible

New Daylight contributors use a range of Bible versions, and you will find a list of the versions used opposite. You are welcome to use your own preferred version alongside the passage printed in the notes. This can be particularly helpful if the Bible text has been abridged.

New Daylight affirms that the whole of the Bible is God's revelation to us, and we should read, reflect on and learn from every part of both Old and New Testaments. Usually the printed comment presents a straightforward 'thought for the day', but sometimes it may also raise questions rather than simply providing answers, as we wrestle with some of the more difficult passages of Scripture.

New Daylight is also available in a deluxe edition (larger format). Visit your local Christian bookshop or BRF's online shop **brfonline.org.uk**. To obtain a cassette version for the visually impaired, contact Torch Trust for the Blind, Torch House, Torch Way, Northampton Road, Market Harborough LE16 9HL; +44 (0)1858 438260; **info@torchtrust.org**. For a Braille edition, contact St John's Guild, Sovereign House, 12–14 Warwick Street, Coventry CV5 6ET; +44 (0)24 7671 4241; **info@stjohnsguild.org**.

Comment on *New Daylight*

To send feedback, please email **enquiries@brf.org.uk**, phone **+44 (0)1865 319700** or write to the address shown opposite.

Writers in this issue

Amy Boucher Pye is a writer and speaker who runs the *Woman Alive* book club. She's the author of the award-winning *Finding Myself in Britain* (Authentic, 2015) and *The Living Cross* (BRF, 2016), and has an MA in Christian spirituality from Heythrop College, University of London. Find her at **amyboucherpye.com**.

Tim Heaton is an Anglican priest in parish ministry in north Dorset. He is the author of two Lent courses, *The Naturalist and the Christ* (Circle Books, 2011) and *The Long Road to Heaven* (Circle Books, 2013). You can connect with him at **facebook.com/lentcourses**.

Liz Hoare is an ordained Anglican priest and teaches spiritual formation at Wycliffe Hall, Oxford. Her interests lie in the history and literature of Christian spirituality and their connections with today's world. She is married to Toddy, a priest and sculptor, and they have a teenage son.

Andrew Carroll Jones is the Archdeacon of Meirionnydd in the Diocese of Bangor (Wales). He has written *Every Pilgrim's Guide to Celtic Britain and Ireland* (Canterbury, 2002, 2009), *Pilgrimage: The journey to remembering our story* (BRF, 2011) and *Mary: A gospel witness to transfiguration and liberation* (BRF, 2014).

Michael Mitton works freelance in the areas of spirituality and mission. He is also an Honorary Canon of Derby Cathedral and is the NSM Priest in Charge of St Paul's Derby. He is author of *Travellers of the Heart* (BRF, 2013).

Margaret Silf is an ecumenical Christian committed to working across and beyond traditional divisions. She is the author of a number of books for 21st-century spiritual pilgrims and is a retreat facilitator.

Naomi Starkey is a curate in the Church in Wales, working in Welsh and English across six rural churches on the Llyn Peninsula. She previously worked as a BRF commissioning editor from 1997 to 2015 and has written a number of books, including *The Recovery of Joy* (BRF, 2017) and *The Recovery of Hope* (BRF, 2016).

Veronica Zundel is an Oxford graduate, writer and columnist. She lives with her husband and son in north London. Her most recent book is *Everything I Know about God, I've Learned from Being a Parent* (BRF, 2013).

4

Sally Welch writes...

This time last year I was in the Holy Land, on a familiarisation tour run by a Christian travel company. The aim of the tour was to introduce parish clergy to the sites and situation of the Holy Land so that they, in turn, would be able to lead other groups. As soon as I arrived, late one night after a long coach journey, my heart was captured by the beauty and the history of the place, and torn by the troubles and the conflict that its people and its landscape have suffered.

We stayed on the shores of the Sea of Galilee, in the heart of Bethlehem and by one of the gates of Old Jerusalem. Because of the nature of the trip, we visited a large number of sites – from the Church of the Holy Nativity to the Church of the Holy Sepulchre with many, many churches in between. We also learnt a bit about the complicated political situation in the Holy Land, hearing the stories of some of its inhabitants and sharing their grief at its turbulent history. At the end of our trip, the Christian guide spoke to us passionately about the need to bring more people to this wonderful, troubled land, to show them not only the historic sites but the living towns and cities. 'Come and see' was his message; 'come and see and then maybe you will understand us better.'

This edition of *New Daylight* invites us to 'come and see', but with the eyes of faith rather than a physical encounter. Liz Hoare helps us to explore the importance of place – and Michael Mitton encourages us to consider how it feels to live without place, in exile. Margaret Silf draws us into the experience of contemplative prayer, inviting us to go deeper in our relationship with God, while Naomi Starkey guides us on our journey towards Easter and beyond through the eyes of those who fail to under-stand the message of Jesus, as well as those who do.

As we journey through these next few months, may we see more clearly the footprints of Christ in our lives so that in turn we may show others the Way that leads to love and understanding, calling them, as we have been called, to 'come and see'.

Sally Ann Welch

The BRF Prayer

Almighty God,
you have taught us that your word is a lamp for our feet
and a light for our path. Help us, and all who prayerfully
read your word, to deepen our fellowship with you
and with each other through your love.
And in so doing may we come to know you more fully,
love you more truly, and follow more faithfully
in the steps of your son Jesus Christ, who lives and reigns
with you and the Holy Spirit, one God forevermore.
Amen

Genesis 12—24:
journeying with Abraham and Sarah

Some years ago, Abraham and Sarah's story became special to me when I received an invitation to start a new life in a different country. I pondered the question of becoming a stranger and foreigner as I came to the end of a prayer retreat in Maryland. As I watched the dragonflies hover over the surface of a pond, I read from Hebrews 11 about Abraham's call to go to a new land, and how he made his home there. The words seemed to leap off the page, pulsing with meaning. For some months before, I had met a visiting Englishman, and now we were testing out our relationship, seeking God's guidance as to whether we should commit to each other. Unbeknown to me, God also directed Nicholas to the story of Abraham. Later we would be grateful for these clear signs of guidance, when getting married and my moving to England entailed major adjustments.

There's much to engage with in Sarah and Abraham's story, whether or not you have a personal connection to it. In it we encounter the challenges they faced in following God's call and how they responded – sometimes with grace and obedience and sometimes not. They are heroes of the faith, but they are not perfect, a fact I find comforting. God used them still, making them the father and mother of many nations. Although they were past childbearing years, and although the promise took 25 years to be fulfilled, God didn't let them down.

At this beginning of 2019, perhaps like Abraham you sense God's call that may entail a change in how you live. As we encounter the ways Abraham and Sarah navigated their journey, we can find encouragement in how they followed him faithfully and we can heed the warnings from when they took matters into their own hands. They waited for years for God's promises to come true, wavering at times but ultimately proving faithful.

May we too live by faith, welcoming the things promised from a distance, admitting that we are foreigners and strangers on earth as we long for a better country – a heavenly one – where we will live in a city prepared for us by God (after Hebrews 11:13–16).

AMY BOUCHER PYE

A new start

The Lord had said to Abram, 'Go from your country, your people and your father's household to the land I will show you. I will make you into a great nation, and I will bless you; I will make your name great, and you will be a blessing. I will bless those who bless you, and whoever curses you I will curse; and all peoples on earth will be blessed through you.'

The beginning of the year is a time for fresh starts and perhaps for resolutions. Think of how Abram must have felt when, at 75 years old, the Lord called him to a new life. Perhaps his heart beat with excitement, but maybe he fretted about the depth of changes he and Sarai would face. For when Abram became a foreigner and a stranger, he would live in a tent, not a palace. And in never returning to his home or his people, he would relinquish his inheritance from his father's fathers. Not only would he miss out on any material possessions, but also he would forfeit the accepted family roles, such as caring for elderly relatives. His new life would entail a sacrifice.

The biblical narrative doesn't tell us what Abram thought or felt as he heard God's call. He and Sarai would have to exercise great faith in obeying the Lord, especially his promise to make them into a great nation. For Sarai was 65 years old and unable to conceive. In that day, being childless often brought shame and fear about the future.

However Abram arrived at his decision of how to respond, in the end he obeyed God: 'So Abram went, as the Lord had told him' (Genesis 12:4). He took his wife Sarai and his nephew Lot, along with their possessions, and set off for the land of Canaan. Here at first they would be foreigners, but in time they would call it their home, a place where they could rest and flourish.

Whatever 2019 may hold for us, may we know God's guiding presence.

Lord God, you called Sarai and Abram away from their home and all that was familiar. When I am faced with change, help me to follow you with grace, courage and hope.

AMY BOUCHER PYE

Led by fear

Now there was a famine in the land, and Abram went down to Egypt to live there for a while because the famine was severe. As he was about to enter Egypt, he said to his wife Sarai, 'I know what a beautiful woman you are. When the Egyptians see you, they will say, "This is his wife." Then they will kill me but will let you live. Say you are my sister, so that I will be treated well for your sake and my life will be spared because of you.'... Pharaoh summoned Abram. 'What have you done to me?' he said. 'Why didn't you tell me she was your wife? Why did you say, "She is my sister," so that I took her to be my wife? Now then, here is your wife. Take her and go!'

The #metoo phenomenon exploded in 2017, following the revelations of alleged abuse by Hollywood mogul Harvey Weinstein. It unleashed an outpouring of stories that were shocking, not least because there were so many of them.

Sadly, this form of exploitation of women goes back to the early stories of the Bible. I find the account of Abram in Egypt, where he passes off his wife as his sister, difficult to read. Abram lets his fears override his wisdom when he thinks that her beauty will lead to his death. In effect he gives her as a wife to Pharaoh, thereby allowing their marriage to be defiled. But the Lord intervenes, sending diseases on Pharaoh and his house, and soon Sarai returns to Abram. I wonder how Sarai felt about the string of events?

I respect those who bravely name abuse, especially when the perpetrator holds a position of power over them. I pray that God would empower us to be among those who speak the truth, in love.

'He is the Maker of heaven and earth, the sea, and everything in them – he remains faithful for ever. He upholds the cause of the oppressed and gives food to the hungry. The Lord sets prisoners free, the Lord gives sight to the blind, the Lord lifts up those who are bowed down, the Lord loves the righteous' (Psalm 146:6–8).

AMY BOUCHER PYE

9

Family ties

So Lot chose for himself the whole plain of the Jordan and set out towards the east. The two men parted company: Abram lived in the land of Canaan, while Lot lived among the cities of the plain and pitched his tents near Sodom… The Lord said to Abram after Lot had parted from him, 'Look around from where you are, to the north and south, to the east and west. All the land that you see I will give to you and your offspring for ever. I will make your offspring like the dust of the earth, so that if anyone could count the dust, then your offspring could be counted.'

How Much Land Does a Man Need? is a short story by Leo Tolstoy published in 1886. It recounts a man winning a prize of as much land as he can claim from sunrise to sundown, marking it as he walks from place to place. The man allows his greed to drive him and by the end of the day, when he makes it back to the starting position, he collapses in a heap on the ground. Tolstoy concludes that in the end, a person needs only enough land in which to be buried.

Land and possessions are necessary in life, but can cause conflict, as Abram and Lot discover when they begin to prosper. The land can't support them both, and so a solution of one going one way and the other going the other needs to be sorted. I find it interesting to note that it's Abram and Lot's herders who start to quarrel, not Abram and Lot themselves. Still, they need to figure out how to live peaceably.

Abram seems to have matured since the fiasco with Pharaoh and Sarai, for he puts Lot's needs before his own, offering him the decision of which land to choose. And God blesses Abram, promising that he will have more land and offspring than he can even imagine.

Possessions can drive a wedge between relationships, especially family members. How much better to be like Abram, if we can, and relinquish our rights.

'How good and pleasant it is when God's people live together in unity!'
(Psalm 133:1).

AMY BOUCHER PYE

Courage in conflict

Then Melchizedek king of Salem brought out bread and wine. He was priest of God Most High, and he blessed Abram, saying, 'Blessed be Abram by God Most High, Creator of heaven and earth. And praise be to God Most High, who delivered your enemies into your hand.' Then Abram gave him a tenth of everything. The king of Sodom said to Abram, 'Give me the people and keep the goods for yourself.' But Abram said to the king of Sodom, 'With raised hand I have sworn an oath to the Lord, God Most High, Creator of heaven and earth, that I will accept nothing belonging to you, not even a thread or the strap of a sandal, so that you will never be able to say, "I made Abram rich."'

Having weathered a battle, Abram might have thought he could rest. But another test came along, one that bears parallels to the story of Satan trying to tempt Jesus in the wilderness, as recounted in Matthew's gospel. Here, the king of Sodom, whose enemies Abram has just defeated in order to rescue Lot, approaches Abram and tries to tempt him with earthly riches. This time, Abram trusts in God to provide and doesn't give in. He doesn't want to be beholden to any earthly kings, but wants to depend on God.

Before this test, Abram was strengthened by the bread and wine given to him by Melchizedek, a priest of God. Some biblical commentators see this as Jesus appearing in bodily form, a foreshadowing of the incarnation. I love the idea of Jesus ministering to Abram through the bread and the wine, just as he ministers to us through these humble but sacred elements! Of course, we can't know for certain that this was Jesus, but even if not, we can see how Abram gained from stopping to worship and honour God.

When we face tests or challenges, we can depend on God's grace to strengthen us as we lean on him for courage.

Lord Jesus Christ, help me to look to you for help in times of need.
Help me to put you first always, and remind me of your presence,
that I may not fear.

AMY BOUCHER PYE

Growing in faith

After this, the word of the Lord came to Abram in a vision: 'Do not be afraid, Abram. I am your shield, your very great reward.' But Abram said, 'Sovereign Lord, what can you give me since I remain childless and the one who will inherit my estate is Eliezer of Damascus?'... Then the word of the Lord came to him: 'This man will not be your heir, but a son who is your own flesh and blood will be your heir.' He took him outside and said, 'Look up at the sky and count the stars – if indeed you can count them.' Then he said to him, 'So shall your offspring be.' Abram believed the Lord, and he credited it to him as righteousness.

This encounter marks a key moment in Abram's journey to becoming the father of God's people. Perhaps he felt vulnerable after his interactions with men in power, for God appears with tender words of assurance for him. The Lord also doesn't become cross when Abram reminds him that his current heir is a servant not related to him. Instead, God reiterates the promises he made to Abram, which we read about in Genesis 12, while also revealing more to Abram. He then formalises the covenant through instructions for Abram's required sacrifice.

As God shares about his covenant in increments, so too does Abram move forward step by step in faith, growing stronger in believing God as he follows and obeys him. He's not perfect, and he faces setbacks, but he's credited as a hero of the faith, one who trusts God and believes that God will follow through on his promises.

Our faith similarly will grow and expand the more we follow God, especially as we look back over our days, weeks, months and years, seeing how he has answered our prayers. Perhaps it's an apposite time to consider the year gone by in this light as we enter fully into 2019.

Lord God, though I falter at times in my faith, strengthen my belief in your promises. Continue to help me discern how you are leading me, and help me to follow you.

AMY BOUCHER PYE

Blame and discontent

So after Abram had been living in Canaan ten years, Sarai his wife took her Egyptian slave Hagar and gave her to her husband to be his wife. He slept with Hagar, and she conceived. When she knew she was pregnant, she began to despise her mistress. Then Sarai said to Abram, 'You are responsible for the wrong I am suffering. I put my slave in your arms, and now that she knows she is pregnant, she despises me. May the Lord judge between you and me.' 'Your slave is in your hands,' Abram said. 'Do with her whatever you think best.' Then Sarai ill-treated Hagar; so she fled from her.

Sarai's suggestion to Abram that her servant girl bear him a child can seem jarring to modern ears. In ancient times, however, this practice was acceptable, partly because of their understanding of reproduction. In that day, they understood the man's sperm as the agent that would bring forth a child, with the woman only the carrier. And thus Sarai thought that a child by Abram through Hagar could, in theory, become the rightful heir.

But the result was a mess. Sarai and Hagar's relationship broke down when Hagar exulted in her pregnancy over her mistress. This incensed Sarai and bred discontent between Sarai and Abram, for she blamed him for the problems. He, in turn, simply abdicated any involvement in the matter. The relationships spiralled down negatively, with Hagar running away in dejection.

Had Sarai and Abram trusted God and waited longer, they could have avoided these problems. How often do we, too, take matters into our own hands when we don't see things happening according to what we desire? We can ask God to help us to trust in him and to wait for his working in our lives.

'But blessed is the one who trusts in the Lord, whose confidence is in him. They will be like a tree planted by the water that sends out its roots by the stream. It does not fear when heat comes; its leaves are always green. It has no worries in a year of drought and never fails to bear fruit'
(Jeremiah 17:7–8).

AMY BOUCHER PYE

A new name

'No longer will you be called Abram; your name will be Abraham, for I have made you a father of many nations. I will make you very fruitful; I will make nations of you, and kings will come from you. I will establish my covenant as an everlasting covenant between me and you and your descendants after you for the generations to come, to be your God and the God of your descendants after you...' God also said to Abraham, 'As for Sarai your wife, you are no longer to call her Sarai; her name will be Sarah. I will bless her and will surely give you a son by her. I will bless her so that she will be the mother of nations; kings of peoples will come from her.'

In the ancient Near East, people often changed their names in recognition of a new life event. This happened to Abram some 25 years after the Lord first made his promise of the covenant to him. No longer, the Lord said, would his name mean 'exalted father', but he would be called Abraham, 'the father of many'. God changed Sarai's name as well; no longer would her name mean 'princess', but she would be called Sarah, 'the princess of many'.

Another common practice was to play with words, letters and meanings. Some Bible commentators see the change in their names as even more significant than the promise that they will be the parents of many. The change added an 'h' to their names, a letter that is part of God's name: Yahweh. Thus the addition could mean that they will for ever be part of God's family, and that they are to be like him as far as they are able.

Would you ever change your name? Take some time to ponder what meaning you'd like a new name to convey, as a reflection of how God sees you.

'Whoever has ears, let them hear what the Spirit says to the churches.
To the one who is victorious, I will give some of the hidden manna.
I will also give that person a white stone with a new name written on it,
known only to the one who receives it' (Revelation 2:17).

AMY BOUCHER PYE

Three visitors

The Lord appeared to Abraham near the great trees of Mamre while he was sitting at the entrance to his tent in the heat of the day. Abraham looked up and saw three men standing nearby. When he saw them, he hurried from the entrance of his tent to meet them and bowed low to the ground. He said, 'If I have found favour in your eyes, my lord, do not pass your servant by.'... 'Very well,' they answered, 'do as you say.'... While they ate, he stood near them under a tree. 'Where is your wife Sarah?' they asked him... Then one of them said, 'I will surely return to you about this time next year, and Sarah your wife will have a son.'

Icons can be used in prayer, as embraced by many in the tradition of the Eastern fathers or St Benedict. These unsigned paintings can be a way to move from the visible to the invisible. In 1410, St Andrei Rublev painted the Holy Trinity icon, depicting the story of Genesis 18:1–10, when the three visitors – thought to represent the Trinity of God the Father, God the Son and God the Holy Spirit – came to visit Abraham and Sarah. (You can find images of this icon online.)

The figure on the left is understood to represent the Father, with the figure in the centre the Son and the figure on the right the Holy Spirit. Together they represent an invisible circle, a shape seen as a symbol of perfection with no beginning or end. Also, within the circle, the three heads of the figures form a triangle, a shape often used to depict the Trinity.

It's helpful to think of the Trinity as represented by the visitors to Abraham and Sarah. They come to clarify the promise of the longed-for heir and even give a specific time frame. What seems impossible – a child from parents well past the age of childbearing – will be brought to fruition by the living God.

I invite you to spend some time praying with the help of the Rublev icon.

Father, Son and Holy Spirit, you delivered on your promise to Sarah and Abraham. Help me to trust you in things little and big.

AMY BOUCHER PYE

Bargaining with God

Then Abraham approached him and said: 'Will you sweep away the righteous with the wicked? What if there are fifty righteous people in the city? Will you really sweep it away and not spare the place for the sake of the fifty righteous people in it? Far be it from you to do such a thing – to kill the righteous with the wicked, treating the righteous and the wicked alike.'... The Lord said, 'If I find fifty righteous people in the city of Sodom, I will spare the whole place for their sake.'... Then he said, 'May the Lord not be angry, but let me speak just once more. What if only ten can be found there?' He answered, 'For the sake of ten, I will not destroy it.'

At times, my children enter into negotiations with me, sometimes in order to wear me down so that I will grant their request. When I'm able to say 'yes' to their desires, I do. But at other times, I swiftly close down the negotiations, partly because I can be tempted to give in when I shouldn't.

In thinking about how I feel when my loved ones keep asking things of me, I find it fascinating to read this account of Abraham pleading for righteous people living in Sodom. He approaches God time and time again, asking him to spare the city if 50 righteous people, 45 righteous people, and down to ten righteous people live there. Each time, the Lord says yes (and with no hint of the irritability I can sometimes display). But in the end, God could find only four righteous people, so the city was destroyed.

Yet this interchange between Abraham and God heartens me, for it shows not only the love and mercy of God, but also Abraham's concern for those in a neighbouring city – even one he may not have had much allegiance to, except that his nephew lived there.

What might you ask God for today?

Lord God, you created us to communicate with you. Thank you that I can not only praise you and give you thanks for the many good things in my life, but I can also present you with my requests.

AMY BOUCHER PYE

The joy of laughter

Now the Lord was gracious to Sarah as he had said, and the Lord did for Sarah what he had promised. Sarah became pregnant and bore a son to Abraham in his old age, at the very time God had promised him… Abraham was a hundred years old when his son Isaac was born to him. Sarah said, 'God has brought me laughter, and everyone who hears about this will laugh with me.' And she added, 'Who would have said to Abraham that Sarah would nurse children? Yet I have borne him a son in his old age.'

A couple I know tried to have children for a decade, undergoing medical tests, exploring IVF treatments and looking into adoption. Year after painful year, they tried to have a baby, but all avenues seemed closed to them. At times their faith in God wavered, as they wondered why they were experiencing such deep heartache. Finally they decided to relinquish their quest, asking God to fill their lives with joy in other ways. And laughter hasn't left their house; in fact, it reverberates with it. Their abundant laughter acts as an invitation for others to join them in embracing and experiencing joy.

God brought joy and laughter to Abraham and Sarah through fulfilling the promises he made over 25 years. Though she thought her womb was dead, Sarah gave birth to Isaac, and laughter erupted into a home that had been filled with pain.

Some people claim that laughter promotes healing. They could be on to something, for laughter is an aerobic activity that strengthens the diaphragm and releases endorphins, the feel-good hormone, into the body. I'm not sure if they are right, but why not be open to laughing today more than usual? We can ask God to help us embrace the joyful side of life, even in the midst of painful circumstances. He promises never to leave us.

Father God, when you came through on your promises to Sarah and Abraham, they rejoiced. Help me to find joy, even if I'm struggling. Help me to laugh, knowing that you have created me to experience a full range of emotions.

AMY BOUCHER PYE

Father and son

Some time later God tested Abraham. He said to him, 'Abraham!' 'Here I am,' he replied. Then God said, 'Take your son, your only son, whom you love – Isaac – and go to the region of Moriah. Sacrifice him there as a burnt offering on a mountain that I will show you.' Early the next morning Abraham got up and loaded his donkey. He took with him two of his servants and his son Isaac… Isaac spoke up and said to his father Abraham, 'Father?' 'Yes, my son?' Abraham replied. 'The fire and wood are here,' Isaac said, 'but where is the lamb for the burnt offering?' Abraham answered, 'God himself will provide the lamb for the burnt offering, my son.'

All those years of waiting, and this? God asks Abraham to sacrifice the fulfilment of his promises to make him the father of many nations? We may have this reaction when we read this story, but we see in the text that Abraham simply obeys the Lord's command. No longer does he take matters into his own hands, such as passing off his wife as his sister or fathering a child through his servant. Rather, he heeds the Lord's instructions and sets off for the region of Moriah. He hears God's command, and he obeys.

We also see the loving relationship between father and son. Note how the conversation between Isaac and Abraham mirrors the loving relationship between Abraham and God. Just as Abraham trusts his heavenly Father, so too does Isaac trust that all will be well on this journey with his father.

As you consider the story, think about how it reflects on God the Father, who sent his son Jesus as a sacrifice to fulfil the law. God followed through on the ultimate sacrifice, that which he did not ultimately require of Abraham. He is our good and faithful Father.

'You see, at just the right time, when we were still powerless, Christ died for the ungodly. Very rarely will anyone die for a righteous person, though for a good person someone might possibly dare to die. But God demonstrates his own love for us in this: while we were still sinners, Christ died for us' (Romans 5:6–8).

AMY BOUCHER PYE

A good death

Abraham left everything he owned to Isaac… Abraham lived a hundred and seventy-five years. Then Abraham breathed his last and died at a good old age, an old man and full of years; and he was gathered to his people. His sons Isaac and Ishmael buried him in the cave of Machpelah near Mamre, in the field of Ephron son of Zohar the Hittite, the field Abraham had bought from the Hittites. There Abraham was buried with his wife Sarah.

Many years ago I learned about the practice of asking God for a good death – one that comes at a good time and in a good way. I am intrigued by the thought of seeking a good death, although of course, I won't know how God answers such prayers this side of heaven. An example of a good death is one in which God takes away any fear we may have of dying. I've seen an older friend transformed in this way. After he experienced God's love one day while taking Holy Communion, he no longer dreaded the experience of dying. Rather, he looked forward to living forever with this God of love.

Abraham is one who experiences a good death. He's 'an old man and full of years', who leaves his inheritance to Isaac, the son of the promise. He is buried next to Sarah, who died before him, in the field he bought for her. Although at times they made mistakes, they followed God and brought glory to him.

When you look back over the past days of engaging with their story, what incidents or encounters stand out? If you have time, write down some of your thoughts.

'By faith Abraham, when called to go to a place he would later receive as his inheritance, obeyed and went, even though he did not know where he was going… And by faith even Sarah, who was past childbearing age, was enabled to bear children because she considered him faithful who had made the promise. And so from this one man, and he as good as dead, came descendants as numerous as the stars in the sky and as countless as the sand on the seashore' (Hebrews 11:8, 11–12).

AMY BOUCHER PYE

Acts 6—7: Stephen

The festival of St Stephen follows so hard on the heels of Christmas Day that it barely gets acknowledged. Very often the day is spent recovering from the merriment of the day before, catching up on family visits or hitting the sales as soon as the shops are open. The story of that first martyr is huddled away, so we may miss hearing that marvellous tale of a man so filled with grace that his face shone, a man so filled with faith that he could face his death with equanimity and a man so filled with the love of God that he begs forgiveness for his torturers.

The tale is told that Karl Barth, one of the world's most famous theologians, was lecturing to university students when he was asked a particularly challenging question: whether he believed that God had revealed himself in other religions, and not just Christianity. Apparently Barth bellowed back, 'No, God has not revealed himself in any religion, not even Christianity. God has revealed himself in his Son.'

By his life, death and resurrection, Jesus showed us what God was like. Through his words and actions he showed us also how to live. Stephen, the first Christian to die for his faith, shows us, through his determination to live – and die – in a way that pointed to God, just what it is to be a Christian. In these two chapters we learn how to serve God, how to avoid the pitfalls that are inherent in any group of people trying to live together in community, and the importance of keeping worship as the main priority, rather than the buildings that we worship in. Through the simple story of a new community, we gain an insight into a model Christian group – focused on prayer and worship, but with a heart for all who come to them in need. Through Stephen's deft retelling of the story of the children of Israel, we hear of the danger of prioritising the bricks and stones of buildings over the actual work of living a life of faith. Finally, we are witnesses to the power of God's grace working in and through his people.

Stephen's life is cut tragically short; his witness and example continue to point the way towards God.

SALLY WELCH

A problem arises...

Now during those days, when the disciples were increasing in number, the Hellenists complained against the Hebrews because their widows were being neglected in the daily distribution of food.

In New Testament times, the lot of a widow could be difficult. Deprived of status and income, she would be forced to rely on her children or close relatives to support her. If she had no such relatives or was living too far from her native land, she would have to look elsewhere for food and lodging. Traditionally the Jewish temple would have offered her such things; when they converted to Christianity it would be from the church that widows and orphans would seek the necessities of life.

In the church of Jerusalem, this was very much the case and the growing numbers of Christians strained not just the church's resources, but also how such resources were distributed. As is normal in all communities, arguments arose over perceived injustices – as the followers of different traditions were accused of favouritism towards their own. Whether or not their widows were genuinely neglected, bitter feelings soon developed.

So often we observe the growth of such divisions in our own churches today! Small incidents, magnified by pre-existing prejudice, worsened by lack of communication, can develop into divisions that threaten the unity of the whole. We must all, as individuals and as communities, be aware of our prejudices and work to overcome them. We must be prepared to look beyond our own interests and see the bigger picture, seeking solutions that are best for the whole community and thus for the kingdom.

At the beginning of this new year, reflect on your own worshipping community. How can you help to maintain the enthusiasm of Christmas services over the next year? How can you as an individual work to heal division within your community? What sorts of self-interest or prejudice might you have to set aside?

Heavenly Father, I give myself to you this day as an agent of your peace. Work through me, I pray, to resolve conflict so that we can live in harmony with you and each other.

SALLY WELCH

... and is resolved wisely.

And the twelve called together the whole community of the disciples and said, 'It is not right that we should neglect the word of God in order to wait at tables. Therefore, friends, select from among yourselves seven men of good standing, full of the Spirit and of wisdom, whom we may appoint to this task, while we, for our part, will devote ourselves to prayer and to serving the word.'

What an example this passage sets! How wise of the twelve leaders of the church to realise that the very nature of their success, the growing number of disciples, also has the potential to be the means of their destruction. For over-preoccupation with the practical aspects of leading a church community, however vital those aspects are for the well-being of everyone involved, is a dangerous road to follow. If all the attention and energy of the leaders were to be focused on providing food and support for the disciples, then very soon the community would become no more than simply another welfare agency. That which lies at the heart of ministry – the call to teach and to pray – must be preserved at all costs if the vitality and true nature of the church is to develop and grow.

The community is called to appoint those with particular gifts of service and administration to take on the practical tasks. These seven men must be not only skilled at what they do but also 'full of the Holy Spirit' – their task is a holy one and requires spiritual wisdom as well as earthly management skills. In this way the time and energy of the twelve will be freed to allow them to 'pray and serve the word'.

Today we must also take care to balance the practical aspects of leading a Christian life with our spiritual obligation to put worship and prayer at the heart of who we are and what we do. We must avoid the trap of becoming so involved in the ministry of service to others, in tasks that involve 'doing', that we forget simply that of 'being' – of dwelling in Christ, reminding ourselves of his love and sharing that love with others.

Lord, teach us to pray – and then to serve.

SALLY WELCH

Growing in faith

The word of God continued to spread; the number of the disciples increased greatly in Jerusalem, and a great many of the priests became obedient to the faith.

Go into any Christian bookshop or study the bookshelves of any Christian training college or the library of a church leader, and chances are there will be a sizeable section on the topic of church growth and how to achieve it. In the western world we are reminded almost daily that church membership is ageing and shrinking; dire predictions of the end of the Christian church in Europe are frequent. Occasional bright spots, such as the growth in numbers of those worshipping in cathedrals or the popularity of 'megachurches' in some large towns, cannot mask the falling number of regular worshippers. How far we seem to have come from those early, joyous days in Jerusalem, when despite fierce opposition from the authorities resulting in almost constant persecution, the 'number of the disciples increased greatly'.

How did they do this? The answer may lie in the few verses prior to today's passage – their attention was focused on prayer and the word of God. Everything else that the new communities achieved flowed from that primary task of 'dwelling in the Word'. All the social support, the acts of loving service, the help offered to the poor, sprang from the original source of the love of God for each individual, accessed by a close and constant relationship with Christ.

The challenges facing churches and Christian communities are complex and demanding – a simple formula will not provide the solution. But if we hold in our hearts the basic principles demonstrated in these few verses, and if we devote ourselves to their practice, then we will grow, both as individuals and as communities. We may not grow in numbers – external circumstances beyond our control may prevent that – but we will grow in faith, in confidence and in love. Such demonstrations of Christ-filled living will surely provide a light in the midst of the darkness of contemporary society that will be a source of comfort to many.

How can you grow in faith today?

SALLY WELCH

'Full of grace and power'

Stephen, full of grace and power, did great wonders and signs among the people.

Our first glimpse of Stephen is of a charismatic leader and speaker, with one additional quality – grace. The Oxford English Dictionary defines the noun 'grace' as 'smoothness and elegance of movement', 'courteous good will' and 'the free and unmerited favour of God, as manifested in the salvation of sinners and the bestowal of blessings'. We all possess the gift of grace – forgiveness of our sins; freedom from fear of the consequence of our evil acts; the promise of eternal life. Perhaps what makes Stephen stand out is his joyous acknowledgement of this gift and his enthusiasm for using it to serve the people he lived among.

I have met people whose lives seemed to be not only grace-filled but also characterised by an outpouring of that grace. These rare individuals are distinguished by the almost luminous expression on their faces, almost a transparency through which the love of God for them and their love for others shines like a light. These people are truly 'graceful'; their confidence in the goodness of God's purposes for them gives them calmness of movement and speech that echoes their inner certainty.

I have also worked with a grace-filled congregation – one that had the self-confidence to reach out and invite others to share their space, providing a supportive environment in which those exploring their faith could learn and discover. I have witnessed the power of such a congregation in shaping for the good the community beyond its walls, through both corporate initiatives freely offered and the work of individuals among the young and the elderly, the sick and the lonely. The 'signs and wonders' performed by such individuals and churches might not be as dramatic as Stephen's, but they are powerful witnesses to the wonder of grace.

'Through many dangers, toils and snares,
I have already come;
'Tis grace that brought me safe thus far,
And grace will lead me home' ('Amazing Grace', John Newton, 1779).

SALLY WELCH

'The face of an angel'

Then some… stood up and argued with Stephen. But they could not withstand the wisdom and the Spirit with which he spoke… They stirred up the people as well as the elders and the scribes; then they suddenly confronted him, seized him, and brought him before the council. They set up false witnesses who said, 'This man never stops saying things against this holy place and the law; for we have heard him say that this Jesus of Nazareth will destroy this place and will change the customs that Moses handed on to us.' And all who sat in the council… saw that his face was like the face of an angel.

Of course, the early church did not have it all its own way in Jerusalem. Some people bitterly resented the vibrancy of these new communities and felt threatened by the increasing number of Christ-followers. At first they tried to defeat them in argument, but spokesmen such as Stephen were so filled with the Spirit and wisdom that their own arguments were overwhelmed. So they decided to resort to subterfuge. In New Testament times, the laws of blasphemy were far reaching and included any derogatory words spoken against God or his power. Stephen's enemies worked hard among the inhabitants of Jerusalem, secretly stirring them up, whispering words against him until the momentum was such that a mob was raised. This mob seized Stephen and dragged him before the council.

The cleverness of the enemies of Christ lies in the subtlety of the witness made against him. Stephen is accused of saying that Jesus will destroy the temple. Jesus does indeed say the temple will be destroyed, but not that he would be its destroyer (John 2:19). Jesus did alter the customs of Moses – but only when they went against the laws of God (Luke 6:9). Such half-truths are the most difficult to withstand, yet Stephen is so filled with grace that he shines (v. 15). So may we seek and find the truth in God.

'The Lord has promised good to me,
His hope my word secures;
He will my shield and portion be,
As long as life endures' ('Amazing Grace', John Newton, 1779).

SALLY WELCH

A surprising beginning

'The God of glory appeared to our ancestor Abraham when he was in Mesopotamia, before he lived in Haran, and said to him, "Leave your country and your relatives and go to the land that I will show you." Then he left the country of the Chaldeans and settled in Haran. After his father died, God had him move from there to this country in which you are now living. He did not give him any of it as a heritage, not even a foot's length, but promised to give it to him as his possession and to his descendants after him, even though he had no child.'

Stephen begins his speech to the people in a surprising way for one who is on trial for his life. Instead of launching immediately into a justification of his own actions, or a description of the death and resurrection of Christ, he begins with a common ancestor – Abraham. He reminds the people who are his accusers that the story of the Jewish people is one of hardship and risk, courage and faith. He shares with them the journey of Abraham, who at the word of God willingly lets go of the security and prosperity that he is enjoying in the land of Mesopotamia to go and settle in Haran. Even then Abraham is not allowed to put down roots, for after the death of his father he is once more enjoined to uproot himself and set off on a journey. At the word of God, Abraham leaves behind the life that he carefully built for himself in his new country and instead faces the unknown once more. So, powerfully, Stephen reminds his accusers of the courage that is needed to live in faith, dependent not on material wealth or even the company of relatives and friends, but solely on the promises of God.

How many times in our lives have we drawn back from taking risks in the name of Christ? Just as Abraham did, we must trust in God and step out boldly, wherever he leads us, reliant on the promises of his presence.

'Come, follow me' (Mark 10:21).

SALLY WELCH

Examples of faith

'Then Joseph sent and invited his father Jacob and all his relatives to come to him, seventy-five in all; so Jacob went down to Egypt. He himself died there as well as our ancestors, and their bodies were brought back to Shechem and laid in the tomb that Abraham had bought for a sum of silver from the sons of Hamor in Shechem.'

The story of God's chosen people is not straightforward or easy. Stephen recounts how Joseph is sold into slavery and goes from there to prison, wrongly accused as Stephen himself has been. But he keeps faith and does not allow injustice or harsh treatment to alter his faith or his determination to live an honest and upright life as he works diligently for his master. This behaviour is rewarded as it enables him not only to save his family from starvation but also to bring them to live with him in peace and prosperity. It seems, however, as if the dream of the promised land is a distant one – the children of Israel are farther from it than ever. But still Joseph and his people keep their faith in God's covenant, and on his death Joseph is buried in the country promised to them by God in a plot of land bought by Abraham.

So too in our lives it may seem as if the promises of God are far from being fulfilled. Times of illness or unhappiness occur, incidents and situations that threaten our belief in God's loving presence and steal away our confidence in his loving purposes for us. Then we must remind ourselves that we are keepers of God's covenant and must, like Joseph, hold on to this during times of doubt and darkness.

---

*'I noticed that during the saddest and most troublesome times of my life,
there was only one set of footprints. I don't understand why,
when I needed you the most, you would leave me.
"My precious, precious child, I love you and I would never leave you.
During your times of trial and suffering, when you see only one set
of footprints in the sand, it was then that I carried you"'
('Footprints', author unknown).*

SALLY WELCH

God's good purposes

'But as the time drew near for the fulfilment of the promise that God had made to Abraham, our people in Egypt increased and multiplied until another king who had not known Joseph ruled over Egypt. He dealt craftily with our race and forced our ancestors to abandon their infants so that they would die. At this time Moses was born, and he was beautiful before God. For three months he was brought up in his father's house; and when he was abandoned, Pharaoh's daughter adopted him and brought him up as her own son. So Moses was instructed in all the wisdom of the Egyptians and was powerful in his words and deeds.'

Despite the faith that Joseph and his sons have placed in the promises of God with regard to the land that he will give them, the deliverance of the children of Israel is still a long way off. Indeed, the situation worsens as the large numbers of Hebrew children born in Egypt are perceived as a threat to the stability of the government. As he continues to recount the story of the children of Israel, Stephen shows how the most unlikely circumstances contain the seeds of God's promises for the future. It is the daughter of their oppressor who rescues Moses, the one who will lead them safely to the promised land. Moses, himself a most unlikely leader, will guide them through the Red Sea and across the desert.

There are times when we look back over our lives and are astonished at where our paths have led. Experiences we might never have expected, people we were unlikely to meet, situations we encountered that could not possibly have been predicted. Yet how often is it that through these very same incidents and events most learning has occurred. How often has the unexpected returned the most benefit and the unusual become the most enjoyable or profitable.

Heavenly Father, help me to recognise your presence in all my circumstances. Help me to live faithfully even when I do not understand my situation. Help me to believe in the promised land, which is life in Christ.

SALLY WELCH

Taking notice

'Now when forty years had passed, an angel appeared to him in the wilderness of Mount Sinai, in the flame of a burning bush. When Moses saw it, he was amazed at the sight; and as he approached to look, there came the voice of the Lord: "I am the God of your ancestors, the God of Abraham, Isaac, and Jacob." Moses began to tremble and did not dare to look. Then the Lord said to him, "Take off the sandals from your feet, for the place where you are standing is holy ground."'

The art of noticing our surroundings is in grave danger today. People walk the streets of their cities, towns and villages with their eyes fixed on their phones, either exchanging conversations with others who are miles away or using mapping applications to find their way around. Cocooned from their environment by a bubble of technology, the features of the landscape pass them unnoticed. Not for them the joy of noticing the unusual, the distinctive, the quirky elements of their surroundings, elements that can add joy and interest as well as increasing our wisdom and understanding.

Even those of us without mobile phones can be too distracted by our inner thoughts to pay much attention to what is around us. What a learning point is to be found, therefore, in Stephen's reminder that if Moses had not stepped aside to examine the burning bush, to explore and marvel at its strangeness, he would not have heard the voice of the Lord.

But this is not all, for before God gives Moses instructions for his new path, he tells him to take off his sandals, because he is on 'holy ground'. To Stephen's listeners, jealously anxious to preserve the sacred aspects of their temple, careful that it should not be 'harmed' by blasphemy, this is a reminder that the entire world is holy, because it is a creation of God, and that anywhere is special that facilitates an encounter between God and his children. Perhaps this is a lesson we too, in our anxiety for the future of our church buildings, should take to heart.

Lord, help me to remember that now, here, I stand on holy ground.

SALLY WELCH

Revelling in the work of their hands

'Our ancestors were unwilling to obey him; instead, they pushed him aside, and in their hearts they turned back to Egypt, saying to Aaron, "Make gods for us who will lead the way for us; as for this Moses who led us out from the land of Egypt, we do not know what has happened to him." At that time they made a calf, offered a sacrifice to the idol, and revelled in the works of their hands.'

Moses has faithfully and bravely delivered God's people from slavery and led them out of Egypt. With all the evidence of past events it would seem only natural for them to follow him where he led them, whatever the landscape, however harsh the circumstances. However, human beings are frail and frightened; we quickly lose our nerve and cling on to whatever scraps of superstition and false hope we can find. So, in the absence of Moses, who has ascended the mountain to receive what will become the laws of the Jewish people, those left below cast around for something concrete on which to rest their hopes. Once they have strayed away from the path, idolatry becomes almost inevitable and the famous golden calf is the result.

Stephen tells this story to remind his listeners that Jesus, like Moses, is their true leader and redeemer, leading them out of the slavery of sin and death. However, he too has been rejected out of fear and unwillingness to embrace the new. Following on from this rejection of truth comes the embrace of falsehood – in this case the sinful idolatry of the Jewish temple, which has, in Stephen's eyes, become the focus of their worship rather than God.

Following Christ is a risky business, and the temptation to turn aside and seek comfort in the material, such as the day-to-day operation of the church building, the administration of the community or the development of a group of people who rely on their own wisdom and experience, is strong. But we need to continue to step out boldly, following only Jesus, relying solely on his strength to sustain us.

'O let me see Thy footprints, and in them plant mine own;
My hope to follow duly is in Thy strength alone' (John Bode, 1868).

SALLY WELCH

The independence of God

'[The tent of testimony] was there until the time of David, who found favour with God and asked that he might find a dwelling-place for the house of Jacob. But it was Solomon who built a house for him. Yet the Most High does not dwell in houses made by human hands; as the prophet says, "Heaven is my throne, and the earth is my footstool. What kind of house will you build for me, says the Lord, or what is the place of my rest? Did not my hand make all these things?"'

In Stephen's retelling of the story of the children of Israel, he reminds them that David was not allowed to build a temple to God, but that God chose Solomon to do so. Stephen thus reminds his listeners that God takes the initiative and will not be dependent on human beings, even for worship. In doing so, Stephen refutes the accusation that he has blasphemed against God and 'this holy place' (Acts 6:11, 13). He does, however, emphasise the fact that the primary purpose of the temple is to worship God, who is the creator of all things. It is not for the self-glorification of its builders, nor is it to be an object of worship in itself.

Thousands of years later, we can use this passage to remind ourselves of the same thing. Church buildings can be wonderful spaces for prayer – they offer us a place of peace and sanctuary, community and relationship. They can be the beating heart of a community, offering support and welcome, a place to encounter God and our fellow human beings. However, we must be mindful that although we may need our church buildings to facilitate our worship, God does not. The all-powerful creator, we are reminded, has heaven as his throne and the earth as his footstool; anything we offer is only giving back what is already his. This thought can help us in our reflections, by keeping buildings of brick and stone in their due place.

Consider the building you pray in most often. In what ways does this building help you to worship God? How might it act as a barrier between you and God?

SALLY WELCH

Faith is not a 'pick and mix' affair

'You stiff-necked people, uncircumcised in heart and ears, you are for ever opposing the Holy Spirit, just as your ancestors used to do. Which of the prophets did your ancestors not persecute? They killed those who foretold the coming of the Righteous One, and now you have become his betrayers and murderers. You are the ones that received the law as ordained by angels, and yet you have not kept it.'

There is a story about John Newton, the notorious slave trader who found faith in the middle of a storm at sea and became a devout Christian. Newton was discussing heaven one day with a long-standing Christian, who asked him what he thought would surprise him when he got there. Newton considered and then replied that first he would be surprised at the people who were in heaven whom he never expected to be there, and then he would be surprised at the absence of those devout churchgoers who he thought would. But the greatest surprise would be his own presence, given that he was such a sinner and reprobate!

Stephen turns from accused to accuser, as he directs his rage at those judging him. Again and again, he says, the people have persecuted those who stood up for righteousness, who reminded their people of God's law and warned them of the consequences of ignoring it. Throughout history, the children of Israel have chosen which rules to obey and which to let slide, imprisoning those who opposed them. Now they have betrayed and murdered the Messiah. They are the ones who should be on trial, not he.

It is a grave trap for the unwary – that of choosing our own rules for living. How easy it would be simply to follow those commands with which we are in sympathy; how easy to stand in judgement over others who do not fit in with our ways of thinking and acting. But judgement is God's alone – we all stand condemned before him, and yet all are saved through the same grace that rescued John Newton.

''Twas grace that taught my heart to fear,
And grace, my fears relieved;
How precious did that grace appear
The hour I first believed' ('Amazing Grace', John Newton, 1779).

SALLY WELCH

Looking upwards

When they heard these things, they became enraged and ground their teeth at Stephen. But filled with the Holy Spirit, he gazed into heaven and saw the glory of God and Jesus standing at the right hand of God. 'Look,' he said, 'I see the heavens opened and the Son of Man standing at the right hand of God!' But they covered their ears, and with a loud shout all rushed together against him.

One of my strongest childhood memories is sitting on the floor of the living room on wet winter Sundays watching the afternoon film. Earlier in the day there would have been church, then lunch, then a long walk in the woods, till finally we were allowed to sit down together and enjoy a movie. These black-and-white films made a terrific impression on me; I would become immersed in the story, usually a western or a war film, and have to shake myself mentally when it was over in order to return to real life.

   Looking back on these films, made in the 1940s and 1950s, it seems to me that they all shared a similar viewpoint on life – that those who lived lives to be proud of (whether they lived or died) did so because they had a cause or a goal that was bigger than they were. It was this awareness that gave them the strength to make the sacrifices or right the injustices that they did. The image of Stephen gazing into the heavens and seeing the glory of God takes me straight back to those noble men and women, fixing their hearts and minds to do what is right, whatever the cost, setting an example for future generations.

   Our lives are made up of many decisions, both those taken every day and those about the direction of our lives. We must pray that these choices lead to lives we can be proud of. Stephen was granted a vision to sustain and support him; when we face difficult choices we may not experience this. However, we have been given the promise that wherever we are and whatever we do, God will be with us.

'And surely I am with you always, to the very end of the age'
(Matthew 28:20, NIV).

SALLY WELCH

An end and a beginning

Then they dragged him out of the city and began to stone him; and the witnesses laid their coats at the feet of a young man named Saul. While they were stoning Stephen, he prayed, 'Lord Jesus, receive my spirit.' Then he knelt down and cried out in a loud voice, 'Lord, do not hold this sin against them.' When he had said this, he died.

A few simple verses, yet they contain such power! Thus did Stephen die, stoned to death by the angry, ignorant mob that had been stirred up against him by clever men who recognised the power of the Holy Spirit within him and felt threatened. On that same day, a persecution of the Christians began throughout Jerusalem (Acts 8:1). The faithful were scattered throughout Judea and Samaria – but they did not stay silent. Even persecution could not prevent them from sharing the gospel (Acts 8:4). The very act designed to stifle Christianity succeeded only in spreading it.

And of course, there is Saul. Saul who guards the coats of those who need more freedom of movement to throw their stones with more vigour; Saul who helps to drag out the Christians from their houses; Saul who in a moment of epiphany becomes the greatest missionary the world has ever known. Augustine is quoted as saying that 'the Church owes Paul to the prayer of Stephen', for surely it is in the seeds of Stephen's forgiveness that Paul's new life is born.

Out of terror, injustice and persecution come faith, love, hope and the spread of the gospel. So too for us. Let our prayer be that in the challenges and difficulties of our life, we fix our eyes heavenward and look for a glimpse of glory. Let it be that we pray forgiveness for those who torment us and that our lives are an example for those around us. Let us not despair in the dark times but find hope in the mysterious purposes of God, who works for the good of all, all the time, for all time.

'The earth shall soon dissolve like snow,
The sun forbear to shine;
But God, who call'd me here below,
Will be forever mine' ('Amazing Grace', John Newton, 1779).

SALLY WELCH

2 Corinthians: the authority of suffering

What we know as Paul's second letter to the Corinthians is probably his third, or even fourth, communication with them. He had already visited them twice, and what he discovered among them had pained him greatly: tolerance of an immoral sexual relationship, denigration of Paul's own ministry and authority, adherence to false teachers who were trying to undermine what Paul had taught this congregation. There was probably a letter of admonition, which we have lost, in between the letters we have as 1 and 2 Corinthians.

Our second letter revisits the Corinthian church's issues, prior to a possible third visit, but in a more positive light, as there is evidence that they have repented and changed both their thinking and their behaviour. Paul is eager to see evidence of their new devotion to following Jesus in the difficult context of Corinth, an international port and pagan city, where temptations to compromise their beliefs and ethics were rife.

He also uses this letter to remind them of the financial need of the Jerusalem church, for which all the churches were taking up a collection. But the theme that emerges most strongly for me in this letter is Paul's efforts to commend his own validity as an apostle, which others in Corinth have been questioning.

What is striking, however, is that Paul does not justify his work by how 'successful' it has been, but by how much opposition, difficulty and danger he has encountered. His authority lies in his 'weakness', not his strength. Thereby he shows himself a true apostle of Jesus, who conquered by enduring violence against himself and who proved the genuineness of his resurrection body by showing his scars.

We too, like the Corinthians, live in an age that seeks luxury, comfort and instant gratification, and where many interpretations of life and the world compete for acceptance. Our authenticity, like Paul's, may be demonstrated not by our 'trophies', such as how many we have converted, but by our faithfulness in the face of setbacks and suffering.

VERONICA ZUNDEL

When disaster strikes

Grace to you and peace from God our Father and the Lord Jesus Christ. Blessed be the God and Father of our Lord Jesus Christ, the Father of mercies and the God of all consolation, who consoles us in all our affliction, so that we may be able to console those who are in any affliction with the consolation with which we ourselves are consoled by God... If we are being afflicted, it is for your consolation and salvation; if we are being consoled, it is for your consolation, which you experience when you patiently endure the same sufferings that we are also suffering.

I write this at the end of a year in which, less than a fortnight into the new year, I was diagnosed with breast cancer for the second time. I had just completed the first term of an MA course, my son had returned to university after dropping out, and everything seemed to be going fine. Then on Friday 13 January (yes, really!) I got my diagnosis.

The year was a blur of treatment, waiting for appointments and trying somehow to keep going with daily life. Was God punishing me? Had I done something grievously wrong? Many Christians, and others, think this way, and the whole book of Job is a debate on just this issue. But Paul here takes it completely for granted that 'affliction' is something his fellow believers will encounter. So did Jesus, who warned his followers of the cost of discipleship (see Luke 9:57–58 and 14:27–28). There is no benefit, Paul seems to imply, in asking why something has happened – rather, we are to seek consolation from God, and then pass that consolation on to others who are similarly afflicted.

During my second 'cancer year', I received dozens of cards and many offers of support and prayer from friends. Facebook was a lifesaver! And although I had just joined a new church, they too welcomed me and prayed for strength and healing. May all our churches be places where those who are suffering can be held up and loved without conditions.

How have you experienced the 'God of consolation'?
How can you pass this experience on to others?

VERONICA ZUNDEL

How do you smell?

But thanks be to God, who in Christ always leads us in triumphal procession, and through us spreads in every place the fragrance that comes from knowing him. For we are the aroma of Christ to God among those who are being saved and among those who are perishing; to the one a fragrance from death to death, to the other a fragrance from life to life. Who is sufficient for these things? For we are not peddlers of God's word like so many; but in Christ we speak as persons of sincerity, as persons sent from God and standing in his presence.

In medieval Catholic tradition, one way of identifying a saint was that they were said to emit a beautiful scent, the 'odour of sanctity', even when they had been in the grave some time. Perhaps this idea came from taking this passage rather too literally. But we still use the metaphor of smell to indicate whether we think something, or someone, is good or bad: when suspicious, we say 'I smell a rat', while the judge trying the author Jeffrey Archer referred to Archer's wife as 'fragrant'.

What does it mean for us to be vehicles of 'the aroma of Christ'? It doesn't seem to have much to do with how theologically educated we are or how orthodox our beliefs. Rather, it is something about 'knowing' Christ – staying close to him both in our devotional life and in how we live every day. Some, perhaps those who are determined to do wrong, may experience this as a 'bad smell', something that makes them feel uncomfortable. Others will be drawn to it, find something attractive in it and recognise in us the Christ who inhabits us by his Spirit.

This can also be a means of identifying those who proclaim Jesus but do not live as he taught. We may just sense that something does not quite add up. By contrast, 'persons of sincerity' may give us a sense of rightness, of their being 'sent from God'. The author of 1 John urges us to 'test the spirits to see whether they are from God' (1 John 4:1).

'Let our praise to you be as incense' (Brent Chambers).

VERONICA ZUNDEL

Living confidently

Such is the confidence that we have through Christ towards God. Not that we are competent of ourselves to claim anything as coming from us; our competence is from God, who has made us competent to be ministers of a new covenant, not of letter but of spirit; for the letter kills, but the Spirit gives life.

Sometimes I wonder if verse 6 here is the most neglected verse in the whole of scripture. In my youth, the UK was several times subjected to enthusiastic Christians starting campaigns to recall society to the ten commandments. But as Paul reminds us here, we are under the new covenant, not the old. While the ten commandments still have value as a portrait of 'the good life', they are not the heart of the Christian faith.

We are under the new covenant, not the old. We are not under the law of Moses, whether the ceremonial or moral law. We are under 'the law of Christ' (Galatians 6:2), which is not about obeying external rules, but about having the right attitudes and actions written on our hearts (see Jeremiah 31:31–34) by the Spirit of Jesus, who lives in us if we have committed our lives to him. The result is that we live not by guilt but by grace, that God takes our failures and turns them into opportunities for learning to be more Christlike.

In my experience, this is often paid lip service to but less often practised. Preachers can talk about the supposed legalism of ancient Judaism, but then set up a new, often unspoken, set of rules for Christians, designed to keep us toeing the official line. Judgmentalism is rife among us when anyone departs from the consensus. By contrast, Augustine of Hippo wrote 'Love God, and do as you like' – meaning that if we truly love God, we will like the things God likes and hate what God hates. A founder of my Mennonite congregation called this 're-reflexing'; we are to follow the promptings of God's Spirit in our deepest selves, until doing right 'just comes naturally'.

'For freedom Christ has set us free. Stand firm, therefore, and do not submit again to a yoke of slavery' (Galatians 5:1).

VERONICA ZUNDEL

There's glory for you

Since, then, we have such a hope, we act with great boldness, not like Moses, who put a veil over his face to keep the people of Israel from gazing at the end of the glory that was being set aside... Indeed, to this very day whenever Moses is read, a veil lies over their minds; but when one turns to the Lord, the veil is removed. Now the Lord is the Spirit, and where the Spirit of the Lord is, there is freedom. And all of us, with unveiled faces, seeing the glory of the Lord as though reflected in a mirror, are being transformed into the same image from one degree of glory to another; for this comes from the Lord, the Spirit.

Have you ever met an author or politician or even church leader whom you have long admired from afar? Was the meeting a disappointment or a moment of inspiration, a kind of sharing in the achievements or character of that person?

The hope of which Paul has written in the previous few verses is the hope that we will share in a much greater glory than the 'borrowed' glory that made Moses' face shine after meeting with God. In fact, he calls the revelation that Moses received from God 'the ministry of condemnation' – strong language indeed – while God's revelation in Jesus is 'the ministry of justification' (2 Corinthians 3:9). This passage suggests that the Old Testament can be understood properly only if we read it in the light of Jesus. In Jesus, we get as close to seeing the face of God as we ever can be this side of the grave.

But what does it mean to see the glory of the Lord with unveiled faces? I think it may be different for different people. Some find God in silence and contemplation, some in music or art, some in the natural world, some in intense worship, some in meeting the needs of the most vulnerable. Whatever our personal way of encountering God, we need to cultivate it, as it is this that transforms us into people who reflect God's glory.

---

*'"Come," my heart says, "seek his face!" Your face, Lord, do I seek'
(Psalm 27:8).*

VERONICA ZUNDEL

Broken pots

But we have this treasure in clay jars, so that it may be made clear that this extraordinary power belongs to God and does not come from us. We are afflicted in every way, but not crushed; perplexed, but not driven to despair; persecuted, but not forsaken; struck down, but not destroyed; always carrying in the body the death of Jesus, so that the life of Jesus may also be made visible in our bodies... So we do not lose heart. Even though our outer nature is wasting away, our inner nature is being renewed day by day.

Often people shrink from evangelism because they think, 'I'm not a very good example of a Christian.' But if we wait till our lives are perfect to share our faith with others, we will never share it! Paul insists that the 'glory' he is talking about is not based on how successful or virtuous we are. We will always fail, and be battered by circumstances, but we can still witness to the God who loves, forgives and sustains us.

What is described here is a life that is always on the edge, one step from disaster, and yet holding on somehow to the one who holds us in a powerful, eternally reliable hand. Our sufferings are a way of following the suffering Christ, 'carrying in the body the death of Jesus'; just as Jesus was 'glorified' on the cross (see John 12:23), so we attain glory by multiple little 'deaths and resurrections' in our lives.

So even if our lives are full of mistakes, suffering and disappointments, the beauty and faithfulness of God can still be seen through us. In fact, our own weakness may well highlight the power of God to take what is broken and restore it. Leonard Cohen wrote, in 'Anthem' (1992), that it was the flaws or cracks in things that allowed the light to shine through – but it may also be how the light shines out. In Japan, there is a tradition of mending broken pottery with a mixture of glue and gold, so that the mended object, streaked with gold, is more beautiful than ever.

People are more attracted by authenticity than by argument.
How can we be more real in communicating our faith?

VERONICA ZUNDEL

A new world coming

So if anyone is in Christ, there is a new creation: everything old has passed away; see, everything has become new! All this is from God, who reconciled us to himself through Christ, and has given us the ministry of reconciliation; that is, in Christ God was reconciling the world to himself, not counting their trespasses against them, and entrusting the message of reconciliation to us. So we are ambassadors for Christ, since God is making his appeal through us; we entreat you on behalf of Christ, be reconciled to God. For our sake he made him to be sin who knew no sin, so that in him we might become the righteousness of God.

Anyone who watches nature programmes, or the news, will know the world is full of enmity, violence and corruption. The Bible tells us that this is not its ultimate destiny; God's purpose is to reconcile creation with God and bring reconciliation between all creatures.

Many Bible translations render verse 17 as 'if anyone is in Christ, they are a new creation'. I prefer the version above, which tells us that not only are we made new when we give our lives to Jesus, but we also see God's world in a new way, freed from death and decay, full of potential to be what God always meant it to be.

Too often we define ourselves as Christians by what and whom we exclude from our lives and communities. But the ministry God has entrusted to us is not one of exclusion; it is one of reconciliation – to bring peace between humans and God, and among each other.

How can this most difficult of tasks be achieved? First, we have to know that this is our mission, and have hearts that are open to all. Second, there are a growing number of organisations (such as Bridgebuilders, which emerged from the Mennonite community in the UK) that train people in the skills of dealing with conflict. But most importantly, we need the power of the peacemaking God to inspire and equip us to imitate the Prince of Peace.

'And the one who was seated on the throne said, "See, I am making all things new"' (Revelation 21:5).

VERONICA ZUNDEL

Qualifications for ministry

As servants of God we have commended ourselves in every way: through great endurance, in afflictions, hardships, calamities, beatings, imprisonments, riots, labours, sleepless nights, hunger; by purity, knowledge, patience, kindness, holiness of spirit, genuine love, truthful speech, and the power of God... in honour and dishonour, in ill repute and good repute. We are treated as impostors, and yet are true; as unknown, and yet are well known; as dying, and see – we are alive; as punished, and yet not killed; as sorrowful, yet always rejoicing; as poor, yet making many rich; as having nothing, and yet possessing everything.

A Baptist wanting their membership to be transferred to a new church would normally come with a letter of recommendation from their old church, to show they were a member in good standing. For church leaders the standard is higher: the selection board would want to look at their qualifications, former experience and 'success' in ministry, and references from other professionals, as well as to interview them and hear their ideas for helping the church flourish.

What most candidates would not bring, however, is a list of the 'afflictions, hardships, calamities, beatings, imprisonments' that they have suffered! Nowadays we lionise Christian leaders because of how many they have healed, how big their church is, or how many books they have sold. Paul's testimony is of quite a different nature: the evidence he offers that he is called by God is all about how much suffering he has endured.

True, he also lists his own spiritual qualities, but they are qualities that have made his ministry genuine – not a list of his achievements or successes. His reputation is of no concern to him; he cares only that those he has brought to Christ are growing in Christlikeness.

If you are a church leader, how do you feel about this portrait of a faithful minister? Or as an 'ordinary' church member, whom do you know who displays these qualities? How might we cultivate them in ourselves or in others?

Reflect on the last sentence of today's reading as a description of Jesus.

VERONICA ZUNDEL

Strong language

Even if I made you sorry with my letter, I do not regret it... Now I rejoice, not because you were grieved, but because your grief led to repentance... For godly grief produces a repentance that leads to salvation and brings no regret, but worldly grief produces death. For see what earnestness this godly grief has produced in you, what eagerness to clear yourselves, what indignation, what alarm, what longing, what zeal, what punishment! At every point you have proved yourselves guiltless in the matter... In this we find comfort.

The Mennonite tradition, to which I used to belong, takes church discipline seriously, and has the practice of 'shunning' or excluding members from church life if they have sinned grossly and failed to repent. While it is important to challenge each other, all too often this kind of action can be used simply to get people to toe an official line. It is not easy to know when to admonish a fellow believer or, if you are part of church leadership, to know when to take disciplinary measures.

In my congregation we only ever once banned a church member from attendance, and this was out of desperation at his provocative behaviour and constant pushing of boundaries. I am still not sure we took the right action – sadly the man concerned has died now and the church is closed, so the matter will never be resolved this side of the grave. We did, however, feel free to express disagreement with each other and to speak out when we felt someone was making wrong choices or off the straight and narrow.

Paul has had to use strong words, not face-to-face but in a letter, about the egregious behaviour the congregation at Corinth has tolerated. This could have led to their rejecting him as an apostle and going their own way – and indeed they have come close to this. But, in fact, it has had the effect he hoped for: they have realised their mistakes, been saddened by their wrongdoing, and changed their attitude and actions. He has no regret for his admonishment of them.

Lord, teach me when to speak words of rebuke and when to be silent.

VERONICA ZUNDEL

Equal under God

We want you to know, brothers and sisters, about the grace of God that has been granted to the churches of Macedonia; for during a severe ordeal of affliction, their abundant joy and their extreme poverty have overflowed in a wealth of generosity on their part... I do not mean that there should be relief for others and pressure on you, but it is a question of a fair balance between your present abundance and their need, so that their abundance may be for your need, in order that there may be a fair balance.

We've all heard many a sermon about stewardship that was advertised as being about using our gifts and talents but which turned out to be all about giving more money to the church. It seems many ministers are embarrassed to talk about the church's need for money without wrapping it up in something else!

Paul wasn't. One of the main purposes of this letter to the Corinthians was to encourage them to give generously to a collection for the church in Jerusalem, whose members were experiencing the deprivations of poverty. As an example, he cites the church in Macedonia, which in spite of their own poverty and suffering have given abundantly to the same collection. I recall in the early 1980s, when there was a review of giving in the diocese I was then in, it was revealed that the churches in the poorest areas gave more per head than those in the richest. They knew what it was like not to have enough.

This is not, says Paul, about making some poor to make others rich. It is about those who have enough sharing with those who don't – and another time, the giving may be the other way around. It is about equality and fairness, redressing the imbalance of wealth. Here, the call is to churches to do this voluntarily, but given the UK's political and legal system is at least partly derived from Christian practice, I wonder what might happen if we applied the same principles to our tax laws?

'For you know the generous act of our Lord Jesus Christ, that though he was rich, yet for your sakes he became poor, so that by his poverty you might become rich' (2 Corinthians 8:9).

VERONICA ZUNDEL

The measure you give

The point is this: the one who sows sparingly will also reap sparingly, and the one who sows bountifully will also reap bountifully. Each of you must give as you have made up your mind, not reluctantly or under compulsion, for God loves a cheerful giver. And God is able to provide you with every blessing in abundance, so that by always having enough of everything, you may share abundantly in every good work… He who supplies seed to the sower and bread for food will supply and multiply your seed for sowing and increase the harvest of your righteousness.

The Victorians divided the poor into the 'deserving' and the 'undeserving', according to whether they thought a person's poverty was due to misfortune or to bad choices. (They didn't seem to consider whether others' poverty might be caused by their own riches.) It often looks as though we're moving back to the same classification today. Paul instead divides those who give to the poor into the sparing and the unsparing. We should not be looking at the recipients' merits, but at our own generosity or lack of it.

A gift given grudgingly, however, is no gift at all. If we can't give willingly, Paul implies, we had better not give at all. But he adds an incentive to give: the bread we cast on the waters (see Ecclesiastes 11:1) will return to us multiplied. This is not the same as certain TV evangelists who promise that if we give to them we will become wealthy ourselves. Paul does not offer us a luxurious lifestyle. Rather, he predicts that our giving will return to us as a 'harvest of righteousness' – not what we fancy having, but all we need for a godly life. This may not consist of material things at all, but the spiritual resources we need in order to carry on being generous.

Perhaps the key word here is 'enough'. If we have enough, why do we need more? And perhaps our understanding of what is 'enough' will change and develop as we grow in Christ, so that we can manage with less and give more.

'Thanks be to God for his indescribable gift!' (2 Corinthians 9:15).

VERONICA ZUNDEL

Power to enable

Look at what is before your eyes. If you are confident that you belong to Christ, remind yourself of this, that just as you belong to Christ, so also do we. Now, even if I boast a little too much of our authority, which the Lord gave for building you up and not for tearing you down, I will not be ashamed of it. I do not want to seem as though I am trying to frighten you with my letters. For they say, 'His letters are weighty and strong, but his bodily presence is weak, and his speech contemptible.' Let such people understand that what we say by letter when absent, we will also do when present.

Are you a different person in different situations? Do you say things behind someone's back that you would not say to their face? Or express opinions in a letter or online that you would backtrack on in person? I must confess to all of these faults at times. I admire people who are the same no matter what the context or who they are with.

Once more Paul is battling with the opinion the Corinthians have of him, and their tendency to compare him with more 'showy' leaders. Like many writers, he is less confident when speaking (unfortunately, in today's publishing market every writer has to be a speaker too!). But he is careful to point out that he is not prepared to reproach the Corinthians in writing and then flatter them in person. He means what he says, whether face-to-face or via a letter. This is what we would now call integrity.

One thing is obvious, however. Paul is not 'showing a bit of muscle' or throwing his weight around. He wants it to be clear that if he is trying to establish his authority, it is not in order to subjugate his hearers. The gift of leadership God has given him is meant to increase the 'stature of Christ' in others (Ephesians 4:13), not to belittle them and make them toe the line. He is so keen to get this over that he says it twice in this letter (see 13:10).

Where have you seen leadership used to build up?

VERONICA ZUNDEL

Boasting of weakness

Whatever anyone dares to boast of – I am speaking as a fool – I also dare to boast of that… Are they descendants of Abraham? So am I. Are they ministers of Christ?… I am a better one: with far greater labours, far more imprisonments, with countless floggings, and often near death… Three times I was shipwrecked… in danger from rivers, danger from bandits, danger from my own people, danger from Gentiles, danger in the city, danger in the wilderness, danger at sea, danger from false brothers and sisters… through many a sleepless night, hungry and thirsty, often without food, cold and naked. And, besides other things, I am under daily pressure because of my anxiety for all the churches… If I must boast, I will boast of the things that show my weakness.

'My congregation's growing fast.' 'We had ten baptisms last week.' 'Our church has a powerful ministry of healing.' It might not be quite as crass as that, but I suspect we've all heard people recommending their church or their favourite preacher in similar terms. I'm willing to bet, however, that we've never heard a Christian leader justifying their ministry in terms of how often they've been flogged or shipwrecked – or, to bring it up to date, how often their church has been broken into or how they can't afford warm clothes.

And yet this is the 'boast' Paul makes to the Corinthians. While he admits he is 'speaking as a fool', I suspect he is offering an antidote to the sort of self-recommendations made by the false teachers who have targeted this congregation. He is also demonstrating the upside-down values of the kingdom of God, where, as Jesus taught, the first shall be last and the leaders are the servants of all (see, for example, Matthew 19:30; 23:11).

Even where Jesus promises compensation for his followers, as in Mark 10:29–30, he adds at the end, almost comically, those two words 'with persecutions'. Indeed, one could say the most fulfilled promise of Jesus is John 16:33: 'In this world you will have trouble' (NIV). We need not look for opposition or difficulty; if we are practising our faith, it will come.

'Woe to you when all speak well of you' (Luke 6:26). Reflect on this.

VERONICA ZUNDEL

Highs and lows

I will go on to visions and revelations of the Lord. I know a person in Christ who fourteen years ago was caught up to the third heaven – whether in the body or out of the body I do not know; God knows… Therefore, to keep me from being too elated, a thorn was given to me in the flesh, a messenger of Satan to torment me, to keep me from being too elated. Three times I appealed to the Lord about this, that it would leave me, but he said to me, 'My grace is sufficient for you, for power is made perfect in weakness.' So, I will boast all the more gladly of my weaknesses, so that the power of Christ may dwell in me.

You know when people say 'I'm only asking for a friend' because they're embarrassed to admit they have a problem? Paul may be doing something similar here. The second half of today's reading makes it pretty clear that he's talking about himself.

Jews of the first century believed in seven heavens, of which the first was the air around us. It reminds me of my young son asking, 'Where does the sky begin?' After some thought I answered, 'I suppose at the ground.' God is as close as the air we breathe, for 'in him we live and move and have our being' (Acts 17:28). But that is only the beginning – Paul seems to be saying he has been taken far deeper into the reality of God.

Few of us have overwhelming spiritual experiences, and they can't be manufactured. Most of the time we struggle to sense the presence of God just in our everyday lives. Even if we do catch a glimpse of God's glory, this is not a right but a gift, as Paul makes clear. Once again, his 'boast' is tempered by his on-the-ground reality: a mysterious chronic illness, or perhaps a temptation, which he entreats God to take away, but which is there to remind him of his own fallibility.

'I pray that you may have the power to comprehend, with all the saints, what is the breadth and length and height and depth, and to know the love of Christ that surpasses knowledge' (Ephesians 3:18–19a).

VERONICA ZUNDEL

Inspection ready

Examine yourselves to see whether you are living in the faith. Test your-selves. Do you not realise that Jesus Christ is in you? – unless, indeed, you fail to pass the test!… For we rejoice when we are weak and you are strong. This is what we pray for, that you may become perfect. So I write these things while I am away from you, so that when I come, I may not have to be severe in using the authority that the Lord has given me… Finally, brothers and sisters, farewell. Put things in order, listen to my appeal, agree with one another, live in peace; and the God of love and peace will be with you.

Churches, schools and public bodies undergo periodic inspections to make sure they are meeting acceptable standards. It helps if the organisation knows in advance what is expected of them!

These closing remarks sum up the themes of Paul's long and varied letter. He is concerned that his hearers should be living their faith, not just talking about it. He wants his relationship with them to be one of friend-ship, not that of a schoolmaster having to tell off his pupils. He wants them to resolve any conflicts and live at peace with one another, for it is the Prince of Peace they follow.

Organisations, as we have often seen, may have ways of papering over cracks and giving a better impression than is true. I don't think the Corinthians could similarly pull the wool over Paul's eyes. He strikes me as someone who has a nose for what is genuine.

Even if Paul could be deceived, we know that God's eye is on us and our communities continually, not just every few years – on us not to condemn, but to call us continually to the self-giving love that God demonstrated to us in Jesus. 'Examine yourselves' is therefore a timely reminder to all of us. We have a role in discipling each other, but ultimately each believer is responsible for their own conscience.

---

*'If anyone does sin, we have an advocate with the Father,
Jesus Christ the righteous' (1 John 2:1).*

VERONICA ZUNDEL

Psalms 94—107: a community seeks to relate to God

Over the years the psalms have played an interesting part in my life. I well remember as a nine-year-old boy having to learn Psalm 23 off by heart as homework. Then came those years I spent as a theology student and being introduced to their history and their ancient context. As a priest I have encountered them in various situations – liturgical, worship, pastoral and personal. But about 15 years ago I was introduced to an Anglican Benedictine monastic order, and for a while I visited this community regularly. I was fascinated by the way in which the brothers and sisters of that place organised the whole of their daily lives around the recitation of the psalms. Although I had studied the psalms and used them in worship, it was encountering them as a framework to one's whole day that had a compelling grip on me.

We find in them vivid and human expressions of so many ancient and contemporary feelings. Our ancestors of faith who composed these hymns were clearly experiencing life just as we do today. They express feelings of grief, gratitude, intimacy, tenderness, indignation, protest, joy, anger, fear and acclamation. The psalms are read, sung, acted out and recited by Christians and Jews all over the world on a daily basis, but what I encountered in that religious community was that they prayed the psalms carefully and gently throughout each day. And in so many ways the experience of praying is about laying our hearts open to God, giving ourselves totally into God's hands. The prayer we offer is our own experience of the moment with all those human feelings. This is the legacy that we have received from those ancient psalmists.

The reflections that follow seek to explore how contemporary Christians can make part of this Old Testament book their own. Instead of attributing each psalm to a single author I have used the idea of their being community expressions of different human feelings – hymns compiled by real-life ancient communities of faith for gathered communities of worshippers seeking to make sense of their relationship with God and with life itself.

ANDREW JONES

The community appeals for justice

O Lord, you God of vengeance… shine forth! Rise up, O judge of the earth; give to the proud what they deserve! O Lord, how long shall the wicked… exult? They pour out their arrogant words; all the evildoers boast. They crush your people, O Lord, and afflict your heritage. They kill the widow and the stranger, they murder the orphan, and they say, 'The Lord does not see; the God of Jacob does not perceive.'

It has often been said that there is a psalm for any given situation and any human feeling. In my pastoral ministry over the years I have found this to be true. Often in pastoral situations I offer to pray and to read a portion of scripture with a person either struggling or celebrating. In such situations the vast majority of people request a psalm. This is especially the case in situations of passionate expressions of grief or lament. This psalm could be described as one of those many psalms of lament. By praying it we stand alongside an ancient community that is lamenting injustices happening at the hands of evildoers.

The psalm is in two parts. The first part (verses 1–11) is a prayer that God will deal with those people who go about their lives without a single care for God and for other people. The second part (verses 12–23) is a prayer of thanksgiving for the way in which God has helped those appealing for justice.

As one begins to read this psalm one can almost hear and feel the desperation of those pleading for God's help. The community can no longer sit back and simply watch atrocities taking place before their very eyes. It is conceivable that this desperate community assembled in the temple courts to pray passionately that God would hear their cries for help. There is a righteous anger running through their prayer of lament, accusing the evildoers of sheer arrogance as they ignore both God and his ways of righteousness.

Like them, we too appeal to God to gift the world his ways of truth and mercy, which are too often clouded by actions of hatred and oppression.

Lord, let my actions today be infused with mercy.

ANDREW JONES

The community encounters the creator God

O come, let us sing to the Lord; let us make a joyful noise to the rock of our salvation! Let us come into his presence with thanksgiving; let us make a joyful noise to him with songs of praise! For the Lord is a great God, and a great King above all gods. In his hand are the depths of the earth; the heights of the mountains are his also.

As an Anglican priest I very much appreciate the liturgical tradition within which we worship and praise God. The 'drama' of worship is something that appeals to many people, especially its movements, actions, colour, music and so forth. On reading Psalm 95 one can imagine that same appreciation for liturgical drama happening in and around the temple precincts when this psalm was composed.

Some Jewish sources suggest that Psalm 95 was used especially at the beginning of a new year, when God is proclaimed as the creator of all that is. In this sense the psalm is sometimes described as one of the so-called enthronement hymns, which sing God's praises as he begins to reign again at the new year festival and which renew once more his promises of old. Thus God invites his people to become once again the community of the covenant.

Anglican priests are expected to begin each day with Morning Prayer, and many people join them in this early act of worship. Psalm 95 is the daily opening invitatory canticle. Each time I recite this psalm, I feel like those Jews of old singing it at their new year festival just outside the temple sanctuary, preparing themselves for their renewing encounter with the creator God (verses 1–7), and, once they arrive, God challenges them to obey and follow him (verses 8–11).

The appropriateness of this psalm as an act of worship at the beginning of the year or at the start of every new day is striking, as the worship leader – then as today – invites the people to come into God's presence with grateful hearts for having the chance to begin again.

Thank you, Lord, for the gift of this new day.

ANDREW JONES

The community proclaims God's glory

Ascribe to the Lord, O families of the peoples, ascribe to the Lord glory and strength. Ascribe to the Lord the glory due to his name; bring an offering, and come into his courts. Worship the Lord in holy splendour; tremble before him, all the earth. Say among the nations, 'The Lord is king! The world is firmly established; it shall never be moved. He will judge the peoples with equity.'

Today we are back in the temple with the community as they celebrate another festival that proclaims God's glory and his enthronement (v. 10). It is probable that this particular new year celebration lasted for more than one day (v. 2). In this psalm, one is able to feel again the joyfulness with which the community proclaimed God's glory, but on this occasion it seems that the people may have gathered from different parts of the country and even beyond. The psalm opens by addressing not just Israel but the whole world (v. 1) and talks in terms of 'families of the peoples' united by their common belief in a God that had saved them and revealed his glory to them in and through his creation (vv. 7, 13).

But I get the impression in this psalm that these festivals that the people were celebrating were much more than simply commemorating an anniversary. By telling their stories and re-enacting them through movement, symbol and gesture, they were in fact participating in a drama that gave the people an opportunity to renew the very fundamental and original events themselves. In that drama of renewal, God is praised for defeating chaos and is acknowledged as king, who is about to enter once more into his reign. Psalm 96 is determined to proclaim this good news as far afield as possible, and a slightly unusual feature of this psalm is that it seems almost missionary. It challenges the gathered community to make God's glory known throughout the world (vv. 2, 10).

When Christians rediscover this kind of God, then our proclamation of his kingship, either in words or good deeds to others, truly becomes good news today.

What is your favourite good-news story? How could you share it?

ANDREW JONES

The community rejoices that things are changing

The heavens proclaim his righteousness; and all the peoples behold his glory. All worshippers of images are put to shame, those who make their boast in worthless idols; all gods bow down before him. Zion hears and is glad, and the towns of Judah rejoice, because of your judgements, O God. For you, O Lord, are most high over all the earth; you are exalted far above all gods.

Kingship, and specifically divine kingship, is a recurring theme in many of our psalms this week. Indeed, it is a major motif of the whole Old Testament, much of which tells the chequered history of human kings. Fundamentally, the Bible views human monarchs as the earthly agents of the divine kingship of God, who is determined that the world he created is one where justice and fair play exist for all people and not just a few favoured ones. This hope of God's just ways being firmly established on earth becomes focused on the promise of a messiah – an ideal human king who would come, in God's time, to enable God's will to be done fully; that is, to usher in the kingdom of God.

Psalm 97 offers interesting insights into the way in which the community regarded both divine kingship and the actual kingdom of God – a kingdom where things are changing for the better. There are two parts to the psalm. The first part (vv. 1–6) reflects on God's coming and the vivid way in which the community believes that will happen. The second part (vv. 7–12) deals with the effect that God's coming will have on both the community of faith and those outside it. Basically, the coming of God's kingdom will be sweetness itself to those who have trusted in him and followed him faithfully (v. 8), but for the others who have shown no respect for God's ways and God's people it will be a bitter blow (v. 7).

As we pray today to the King of Kings, let us ask for faithful hearts and that, like the community of old who first sang this psalm, ours will be one that stands in solidarity with those who rejoice that things are changing.

ANDREW JONES

The community sings of renewal

O sing to the Lord a new song, for he has done marvellous things. His right hand and his holy arm have gained him victory. The Lord has made known his victory; he has revealed his vindication in the sight of the nations. He has remembered his steadfast love and faithfulness to the house of Israel. All the ends of the earth have seen the victory of our God.

Over the years, commentators have described the book of Psalms as the hymn book of the Bible. I like to think of it as the hymn book of the temple. I expect it was very different back in the days of the temple, but imagine for a moment a family arriving at the temple courts for prayers and, just as we are given a hymn book as we enter a church, the psalter being handed to them in preparation for singing the hymns. So it doesn't come as much of a surprise to see how important a role the temple plays in the theology of the psalms.

During this past week we have been in and out of the temple praising God for his majesty. The people in those days believed that the temple was God's palace and from it God reigned on earth, offering his people blessing, judgement and new life. They went there to encounter God – almost to be granted an audience with him. It is understandable that they were keen to sing a new song to their God, as we do today; it was the natural and joyful way to praise and worship God. In this psalm the reason for offering praise is to thank God for his saving deeds to Israel and the nations beyond (vv. 1–3), and it calls upon the whole world (vv. 4–6) and even the whole of creation (vv. 7–9) to sing with joy.

Today, we ask that same God to renew in us a spirit of thanksgiving for his saving deeds to us, so that we too may sing new songs in our hearts.

What new song will you sing today? How will that be translated into prayer and action?

ANDREW JONES

The community worships God's holiness

He spoke to them in the pillar of cloud; they kept his decrees, and the statutes that he gave them. O Lord our God, you answered them; you were a forgiving God to them, but an avenger of their wrongdoings. Extol the Lord our God, and worship at his holy mountain; for the Lord our God is holy.

Today we come to the last of the so-called enthronement hymns that the community sang to mark the majesty of God and his reign on earth. In several of the psalms some verses are divided by refrains or choruses. Psalm 99 is divided into three stanzas, each followed by a refrain (vv. 3, 5 and 9), the keynote of which is God's holiness. Yesterday we imagined the people being handed a hymn book as they entered the temple courts. Today let's imagine that the temple worship is supported by a choir, who alone sing the refrains.

The hymn itself praises the fact that God has revealed his holiness to the people of Israel. Each of the three stanzas highlight particular aspects of God's holiness – his awe-inspiring power (vv. 1–3), his righteous power (vv. 4–5) and his gracious power and judgement (vv. 6–9). The verses in today's passage remind us of the exodus experience in the wilderness, where God exercised both his judgement and his righteousness and revealed his power by answering the prayers of his people (v. 8), offering them new and just decrees (v. 7) and forgiving or even punishing them (v. 8).

The verses end with one final call for the people to enter the temple to worship, as the people believed it was on that holy mountain that direct encounters with God were possible, thus highlighting his divine presence. Since the early third century the Christian church has also sung of God's holiness in order to proclaim that same divine presence. By singing 'Holy, Holy, Holy' we too encounter that same God of old and prepare for the abundance of kingdom life.

Holy God, stir our hearts today as we come into your awesome presence in which we have freedom to do your will.

ANDREW JONES

The community is a confident people

Know that the Lord is God. It is he that made us, and we are his; we are his people, and the sheep of his pasture. Enter his gates with thanksgiving, and his courts with praise. Give thanks to him, bless his name. For the Lord is good; his steadfast love endures forever, and his faithfulness to all generations.

On Palm Sunday some church congregations have a procession into the church building, during which they sing a hymn and stop at specific places to reflect on Jesus' entry into Jerusalem. Over the past two days we have thought of the psalter as the temple hymn book and have thought of a temple choir; today, let us imagine a temple celebration involving a procession from outside the building into the compound itself. Like church processions on Palm Sunday, this one would pause at specific places to remember God's covenant with his people – at the gates and at the courts (v. 4), for instance.

The psalm begins by asking the people to cry out and sing for joy (vv. 1–2), and one can begin to imagine a procession of confidence, noise, colour, drama, music and chants. The psalm tells us why they were doing this – in v. 3 we notice that the community celebrates the covenant with jubilation precisely because the Lord is God and he has made Israel his own people. The same verse also refers directly to three covenant hallmarks, namely, belonging to God, being God's people and being the sheep of his own pasture. The last verse (v. 5) is a climax to the covenant song, as God expresses his steadfast love and faithfulness as a response to his people's obedience.

How, then, do we respond? Certainly, through the climax of what began with a Palm Sunday procession, we too are confident of that same covenant. Maybe some days we are less able to imitate the first two verses of this psalm with total joy – for all kinds of reasons. But we can imitate the next two verses by offering ourselves anew each day to God's service.

'To know you more clearly, love you more dearly, follow you more nearly, day by day' (Richard of Chichester, 1253).

ANDREW JONES

The community seeks fullness in life

I will look with favour on the faithful in the land, so that they may live with me; whoever walks in the way that is blameless shall minister to me. No one who practises deceit shall remain in my house; no one who utters lies shall continue in my presence.

I get the impression that this psalm is less of a song and more of a conversation. Scholarly opinion claims it to be a dialogue between the king and God. It may be part of a speech that the king gave either at his enthronement or during the celebration of a royal anniversary. It could also have been part of a liturgy at a time of special need or at a service where divine blessings on the king were renewed.

Whatever the original context, the speech is not in any way a detailed report on the state of the nation but is, rather, a brief reflection on his leadership. In many ways it seems that it could have been an attempt by the king to seek God's intervention to help him and his community in response to their fidelity. In the first part of the speech (vv. 1–3a), the psalmist outlines how he rules, and in the second part (vv. 3b–8) he comments on how he expects to deal with those who do not conform to his ways of justice.

For me, this psalm is as much about leadership today and into the future as it is about a king's leadership thousands of years ago. As Christians, we hope for the fulfilling of God's kingdom of peace and justice one day – that is, the model of a world we have been invited to bring about. Christ calls us to strive for justice, compassion and humility in our dealings with others – surely the stuff of a better world.

The king promises that those who walk blamelessly will serve him (v. 6). Blamelessness is to be discovered at the very core of our human and Christian lives where honesty, compassion, justice and humility abide. These are the qualities that make us fully human and fully Christian. Let us pray with this psalm that we rediscover that fullness.

Lord, help me today to be fully human and fully Christian.

ANDREW JONES

The community confesses
to a promising God

He will regard the prayer of the destitute, and will not despise their prayer. Let this be recorded for a generation to come, so that a people yet unborn may praise the Lord: that he looked down from his holy height, from heaven the Lord looked at the earth, to hear the groans of the prisoners, to set free those who were doomed to die.

In contemporary worship, prayers of confession play a significant role. Usually such penitential prayers happen early in the service, to emphasise the importance of approaching worship with contrite hearts – saying sorry to God enables us to create a fertile heart for what is to follow. In some churches there are set prayers of confession that are used by the whole congregation. The same was probably true for Jews worshipping during the time when the psalms were being written, and it is conceivable that Psalm 102 was one such set prayer of confession. It is certainly a psalm that comes from the collection we call the penitential psalms, where the worshipper submits to God's judgement and seeks his pardon and strength.

There are two notable parts to this psalm. First, there is the prayer of lament (vv. 1–11 and 23–28) and, second, there is a hymn tucked into the middle of the prayer (vv. 12–22). Once more the context is one of cere- mony – an act of worship is taking place in which God is addressed by a community acknowledging and proclaiming God's rule afresh and in which the individual worshipper is assured of God's blessing, thus glorify- ing him. The glorification of God is the context of today's passage, and it is striking how the worshipper is keen to record God's gracious acts for the benefit of future generations, as they, in much the same way, will gather to worship and rejoice at God's covenant.

In our own day, we continue to tell that same ancient story so that our identity as Christians may be preserved in a fast-changing world and that the cherished traditions of our church may be protected in difficult times.

How has God been gracious to you this week?

ANDREW JONES

The community gives thanks for God's unfathomable love

The Lord has established his throne in the heavens, and his kingdom rules over all. Bless the Lord, O you his angels, you mighty ones who do his bidding, obedient to his spoken word. Bless the Lord, all his hosts, his ministers that do his will. Bless the Lord, all his works, in all places of his dominion. Bless the Lord, O my soul.

There is something remarkably personal about this psalm, which possibly is why it is many people's favourite. It is spoken by a person who has clearly experienced some difficulties and has found strength through God's grace to discover healing and transformation. He compares what he himself discovered about God to the same discoveries made by Moses and the people of Israel (v. 7). What is distinctive about this great song of praise is the obvious connection between personal experience of God and the way that experience helps to interpret scripture.

The psalm opens with a song of blessing (vv. 1–2), which is followed by a confession of the psalmist's experience of God (vv. 3–5) and the way in which others throughout history have experienced the same (vv. 6–13). The psalm also compares human weakness and divine power (vv. 14–18) and then reaches a climax of personal gratitude for all that God has done (vv. 19–22). What I enjoy about today's passage is that the worshipper recognises that he alone cannot sufficiently express his gratitude, and so he calls upon all of heaven to help him ring out the song of praise.

I mentioned a few days ago that in my own pastoral ministry people experiencing personal difficulties often appreciate hearing a psalm read out. At times of bereavement Psalm 103 resonates powerfully with those who mourn the loss of loved ones, because it places the transience of life firmly within God's faithfulness. For Christians, life is not a game of hit or miss, nor is it a series of mere coincidences; it is rather a powerful journey where our lives and God's faithful love weave together and become a covenant of trust that can be renewed every day through prayer.

Remind me this day, O Lord, that I do not walk alone.

ANDREW JONES

The community reflects on God's exuberance

You set the earth on its foundations, so that it shall never be shaken. You cover it with the deep as with a garment; the waters stood above the mountains. At your rebuke they flee; at the sound of your thunder they take to flight. They rose up to the mountains, ran down to the valleys to the place that you appointed for them.

Today's psalm begins a trilogy of songs praising the beauty and goodness of creation. Interestingly, Psalm 104 is more about the actual physical gift of creation and less about the creator himself, although as the psalm develops, the exuberance of creation is attributed to God and people are given both the privilege and challenge of caring for it. As the psalm ends, the point is made that men and women have received God's creation as a loving gift. This challenges us to accept a responsibility of care and a duty to work alongside God in caring for the world, while not replacing him.

The selected verses for today draw out both the poetic and the reflective aspects of this psalm extremely well. The verses focus on the origin of creation after the waters have been lowered and the mountains revealed. The psalmist's ideas on creation are very different from the way in which we think of the origins of creation today, but we continue to share two things with these people of old: a sense of awe at God's creative power and trust in that power as it is revealed in the ordered creation.

The picture painted in this psalm is one of interdependence and mutual relationship between God's creatures, on the one hand, and between us and God, on the other; there is a deep sense of cooperation between creation and creator. I am reminded of this each time I celebrate the Eucharist and come to the part where the bread and wine are offered – bread that earth has given and human hands have made and wine as the fruit of the vine and work of human hands. Blessed be God for ever.

Heavenly Father, help me to care for God's creation – today.

ANDREW JONES

The community obeys the covenant of old

He is the Lord our God; his judgements are in all the earth. He is mindful of his covenant forever, of the word that he commanded, for a thousand generations, the covenant that he made with Abraham, his sworn promise to Isaac, which he confirmed to Jacob as a statute, to Israel as an everlasting covenant, saying, 'To you I will give the land of Canaan as your portion for an inheritance.'

I mentioned a few days ago the Jewish commitment to remembering and to telling the story. I was once a student in Jerusalem and just before I got there someone told me to climb the Mount of Olives before sunrise and stay there awhile to discover why the hymn 'Jerusalem the Golden' was written. It took me a few weeks to make the journey, as I was a bit nervous and times were not good in Jerusalem then. When I eventually did, I was flabbergasted on arriving at the summit – there were dozens of young men holding their tiny babies and whispering into their ears. I wanted to find out what was going on and plucked up the courage to ask one of them. Immediately came back an astounding reply – they were telling them the story! They were baby-talking Psalm 105 into the ears of their infants as the sun rose to shine on the temple mount.

The psalm begins with a call to worship (vv. 1–6), followed by a reminder of the times when the people wandered landless (vv. 12–15), and then by a long account of their history from the exodus (vv. 16–43) to their arrival in the promised land (vv. 44–45). It is a hymn that proclaims the covenant between God and his people, and was sung as festival pilgrims to the temple rejoiced in the presence of their God, hearing again their story of salvation and retelling it in order to glorify God.

Today's passage comes from the start of the hymn proper, and the theme is the fulfilment of the promises God had made with their ancestors. In it God is always the subject of the actions and the hymn serves to sing of his faithfulness and grace.

Which part of your story would you want to tell the next generation?

ANDREW JONES

The community remembers their ancestors' acts

Both we and our ancestors have sinned; we have committed iniquity, have done wickedly. Our ancestors, when they were in Egypt, did not consider your wonderful works; they did not remember the abundance of your steadfast love, but rebelled against the Most High at the Red Sea. Yet he saved them for his name's sake, so that he might make known his mighty power.

Today we hear more about the people's ongoing covenant relationship with God, but this time with a difference. Unlike yesterday's psalm, today's is not a hymn but rather a community lament. As the people review their history they reflect not on God's great acts but on the way their ancestors rebelled against God despite his love and constant generosity. In yesterday's psalm the people give thanks and are obedient; today the people confess their ingratitude and recognise their disobedience. Or, to put it another way, yesterday we encountered the righteousness and grace of God and today we encounter the sins of the people.

Theologically, and in many other ways, these of course belong together, and one's personal experience of life shows this to be true. Human nature has always struggled with this duality and paradox, and it is this struggle that lies at the heart of the psalm. What is interesting in today's selected verses is that the people don't simply blame their ancestors; instead, they begin by situating themselves in the same place of disobedience. The people even confess that the exodus from Egypt showed not liberation but unbelief and rebellion. Yet God remained steadfastly faithful and did not abandon his people, who regard God's creative and redeeming love with negligence and disdain.

It is not always easy to find the balance between knowing about and trusting in God's grace and how he has worked in our lives, as he did in the lives of the people of the psalms, and living a wholesome life of grace. But it is a balance that we are called upon to rediscover every day.

God gives us grace before he even asks for our faithfulness.

ANDREW JONES

The community testifies to God's redeeming love

Let the redeemed of the Lord say so, those he redeemed from trouble… He turns a desert into pools of water, a parched land into springs of water. And there he lets the hungry live, and they establish a town to live in; they sow fields, and plant vineyards, and get a fruitful yield. By his blessing they multiply greatly, and he does not let their cattle decrease.

This psalm was probably originally in two parts and recited or sung as the community testified and gave thanks before offering a sacrifice, probably at a festival that drew pilgrims from different parts of the world (v. 3). The first part (vv. 1–32) has rhythms and repetitions, giving a sense of liturgy and movement as the officiating priests call the people to offer thanksgiving. The second part (vv. 33–43) is a slightly different kind of hymn, where the pilgrims testify to a God of blessing (v. 38) and offer praise for the privilege of being able to participate in and share God's grace.

In today's selected verses we read the opening of that second hymn. The people glorify God's sovereign rule on earth and recall the way God's power was revealed through events in history. The pilgrims recognise that God's power on earth continues despite life's ups and downs.

As I look back at this collection of psalms we have explored together, my abiding memory will be that these were living hymns sung by real people as they encountered God in their everyday lives. Indeed, these hymns played a significant role in the life of Jesus – he quotes them and as he worshipped in the synagogue he would have heard them sung constantly.

The heart of Jesus' teaching is the same as the heart of the psalms, namely, a song about a creator God who rules on earth, dwells in heaven and rejoices as he continues to gaze at his creation – even at the bad bits we have created – knowing that in his good time it will be renewed and refreshed.

'For God so loved the world that he gave his only Son' (John 3:16).

ANDREW JONES

Contemplative prayer

I walk regularly around my own neighbourhood and know every path and tree along the way, but familiarity, I realise, can make me blind. So every so often I say to myself, 'Suppose you didn't live here, but were just visiting. Look at these paths, these trees, as though you were here for the first time in this present moment. Listen to the birds you hear every morning, and hear them for the first time.' Then I see everything with fresh eyes. I appreciate what I see. I even say 'thank you' for it.

Contemplative prayer is rather like this. It can help us see the world, and the people around us, in a fresh light, revealing the extraordinary within the ordinary and turning our garden hedges into burning bushes. It can open our inner eyes to see more deeply into the mystery of things – to tune in to the pulse of God throbbing through all creation.

I once visited a wild and beautiful place on a remote Scottish island, where sea eagles make their homes. It was easy in such a location to feel close to the divine mystery. Afterwards, in a gift shop, I discovered that someone else had also experienced this sense of the entire wonder of life present in every single part. I found an unusual painting: a perfect image of a sea eagle painted on a feather not more than 10cm long – the whole eagle revealed on one of its feathers. What an amazing piece of art, and what a perfect reminder that the whole of the divine mystery is present in every part of creation.

To enter into contemplative prayer, we need to come to silence and stillness, adjusting our life's pace to the much slower heartbeat of eternity. In an age that demands rapid results and fast fixes, this is countercultural. In a culture that prefers to take an instant harvest from the supermarket shelves, the task of contemplation is the patient preparation of the ground of our hearts for spiritual seeding, so that God can do the growing.

I hope these days of exploration may help you slow down your heart's clock, that you might feel the pulse of the divine presence, moment by moment, sustaining your life's journey.

MARGARET SILF

At home in God's heart

How lovely is your dwelling place, O Lord of hosts! My soul longs, indeed it faints for the courts of the Lord; my heart and my flesh sing for joy to the living God. Even the sparrow finds a home, and the swallow a nest for herself, where she may lay her young, at your altars, O Lord of hosts, my King and my God. Happy are those who live in your house, ever singing your praise.

We can learn contemplation from the humblest of God's creatures. I discovered this one morning on mainland Orkney off the north coast of Scotland, where I was visiting the 5,000-year-old Neolithic chambered cairn at Maeshowe.

The guide led us across the fields and through a low entrance gap into the ancient inner chamber. Human life had ebbed and flowed here through five millennia, its passing celebrated in hallowed ritual, and an awed silence fell as we breathed in the atmosphere of this sacred space.

Silence, that is, except for the occasional rustle of wings, as a mother swallow circled the chamber around her family of chicks, apparently oblivious to our intrusion. She had built her nest in the place that would have been the focal point of the rituals once performed there, and ever since, the guide told us, she was always there in the chamber, focusing on what mattered most – the raising of her brood. She was surely one of God's natural contemplatives, with everything to teach us.

A key component of contemplative prayer is the art of focusing. Some people use a familiar word or phrase, such as 'Maranatha' or 'Come, Lord Jesus', to help themselves come to a focused inner stillness. Others let their gaze rest on an object, such as a flower, or a sacred symbol or image. This keeps the normally over-busy conscious mind peacefully occupied, and allows us to enter a deeper stillness, just as I entered the ancient stillness of the cairn that morning. But it was the swallow who taught me more than any prayer manual could have done. She knew what mattered most, and she allowed nothing to distract her from her holy task.

May my heart stay in orbit around what matters most,
wherever my mind may wander.

MARGARET SILF

Basking in the light

The Lord spoke to Moses, saying: Speak to Aaron and his sons, saying, Thus you shall bless the Israelites: You shall say to them, The Lord bless you and keep you; the Lord make his face to shine upon you, and be gracious to you; the Lord lift up his countenance upon you, and give you peace. So they shall put my name on the Israelites, and I will bless them.

A story is told about a man who used to go into his local church when all was quiet and simply sit at the back and gaze straight ahead. The pastor noticed this and began to wonder whether this silent visitor might be seeking help. One morning he approached the man and asked him gently, 'Is there anything I can do for you?' The man looked up in some surprise and said, 'Thank you, but there is nothing I need. I love to come in here and sit still and I just look at him, and he looks at me.'

This is contemplative prayer – just sitting, gazing into the heart of the mystery and letting the mystery gaze back upon us. No words needed. Today's reading invites us simply to let the light of God shine upon us, bringing grace, peace and blessing. A big ask – yet all we have to do is to let it shine.

If you live in a climate where the sun rarely shines, you will know how eagerly we go out and bask in it when it does, wanting nothing more than simply to soak up the warmth and the light. In countries in the throes of drought, people rush outside when the precious rain falls, just for the joy of being exposed to the life-giving water soaking down to the roots of their being.

Contemplative prayer is rather like this – simply basking in the warmth and light of God's love, simply letting ourselves be drenched in life-sustaining, life-restoring grace.

Quakers speak of prayer as 'holding someone in the light'. No need to verbalise our problems or tell God what needs to be done. Enough just to be held in the light.

To be blessed by God is as simple as letting ourselves bask in the light of God's love.

MARGARET SILF

Windows into mystery

Surely, this commandment that I am commanding you today is not too hard for you, nor is it too far away. It is not in heaven, that you should say, 'Who will go up to heaven for us, and get it for us so that we may hear it and observe it?' Neither is it beyond the sea, that you should say, 'Who will cross to the other side of the sea for us, and get it for us so that we may hear it and observe it?' No, the word is very near to you; it is in your mouth and in your heart for you to observe.

At this time of the year readers in the northern hemisphere can look out at the natural world and see the deciduous trees still closed up in the sleep of winter. Soon the new buds will sprout and the branches gradually transform into springtime green. As the temperature rises, the flowers will emerge, and, in the fullness of time, the fruits. If we had never seen this miracle before, could we believe that all this new life is already there inside the tree that looks so lifeless?

And suppose we found caterpillars eating our cabbages in the garden, and someone were to tell us that there is a butterfly inside each one of them. Would we believe it? If we didn't know the whole story, wouldn't we think that maybe the leaves, flowers and fruit were deposited on the tree by some outside agency? Would we not think that the butterfly had flown in from some exotic land?

Contemplative prayer opens a window into that deep interior, inviting us to catch a glimpse of the fruit inside the tree, the butterfly inside the caterpillar and, most amazingly, the fullness of the kingdom of God latent inside our own hearts, awaiting the fullness of time, and grace, for its flowering. We can't force it. We can't even imagine it. But we are invited to believe in it, and to nourish it in the silence of contemplation – the seed-bed and the nursery of divine transformation.

May we learn to stop our frantic search for the kingdom, so that we can become still and know its reality deep within us and all around us.

MARGARET SILF

Rooted in God

Happy are those who do not follow the advice of the wicked, or take the path that sinners tread, or sit in the seat of scoffers; but their delight is in the law of the Lord, and on his law they meditate day and night. They are like trees planted by streams of water, which yield their fruit in its season, and their leaves do not wither. In all that they do, they prosper.

Trees are great teachers. Among many other things we learn from them, as in today's reading, is the fact of the intimate connection between the roots and branches, each depending on the other for the fullness of life. This surely applies not just to trees but also in our own lives. The branches of our outer lives can never thrive if the roots of our inner lives are not planted deep in the soil that both sustains them and gives them stability and a place of belonging.

The psalmist reveals that the tree whose roots go deep into the living water will survive the dry seasons and bring forth leaves and fruit in due time. Those whose lives are planted in God will likewise bear spiritual fruit.

This connection reminds me of an oil lamp. One end of the wick must be immersed in the oil and the other end extended into the world, otherwise there will be no light. The same is true for us. Our lives, ideally, are both contemplative and active. If they are to bear fruit, we must ensure that our hearts remain immersed in God, while our lives also branch out into the world, bearing fruit. All contemplation and no action means that, however faithful and intense our prayer, it will not find expression in the wider world. All action and no contemplation means that any fruit our lives might bear will quickly wither for lack of deep sustenance.

Happy the pilgrim who, like the tree in the psalm, finds a balance between contemplation and action, for that pilgrim's life shall bear fruit that will nourish a spiritually starving world.

May our deep invisible roots remain immersed in the ocean of God's love, so that the branches of our lives may survive the drought and bear fruit for the nations.

MARGARET SILF

The gift of the dewfall

I will heal their disloyalty; I will love them freely, for my anger has turned from them. I will be like the dew to Israel; he shall blossom like the lily, he shall strike root like the forests of Lebanon. His shoots shall spread out; his beauty shall be like the olive tree, and his fragrance like that of Lebanon. They shall again live beneath my shadow, they shall flourish as a garden; they shall blossom like the vine, their fragrance shall be like the wine of Lebanon.

'Dew' is a beautiful, gentle word. In today's reading God promises to fall like dew upon Israel. And the result will be a blossoming forth and fruitful flourishing, and the emergence of fresh new growth from deep roots, as far-reaching and majestic as the forests of Lebanon.

I was once visiting the cemetery of a convent in south Wales, reflecting on the life of a sister whom I knew and who had recently died and been buried there. It was early morning and the rising sun shone down, causing the dewdrops on the grass to shine like diamonds.

It felt to me at that moment that God was offering me a diamond in a dewdrop and, with that, the sense of an invitation to make a choice: what would I prefer, if I could choose – a precious, sparkling diamond or a precious, sparkling dewdrop?

My response to this unspoken question was clear. I would choose the dewdrop. The diamond would, of course, be very valuable and very beautiful, while a dewdrop would be gone by midday. However, the dewdrop would, by midday, have soaked deep into the dry earth and helped to make it a little bit more fruitful. I wanted my life to be like that. Contemplative prayer is like this – not a gem to be kept in a showcase, but a drop of life itself, soaking into our hearts and bringing forth new growth.

Diamonds may be a girl's (and boy's) best friend, but a drop of dew carries the source of life itself. When it comes to a choice, really there is no contest.

May the presence and power of God soak deep into our hearts like dew and grow shoots of love and compassion in our lives.

MARGARET SILF

Burning bushes in the park

Moses was keeping the flock of his father-in-law Jethro, the priest of Midian; he led his flock beyond the wilderness, and came to Horeb, the mountain of God. There the angel of the Lord appeared to him in a flame of fire out of a bush; he looked, and the bush was blazing, yet it was not consumed. Then Moses said, 'I must turn aside and look at this great sight, and see why the bush is not burned up.' When the Lord saw that he had turned aside to see, God called to him out of the bush, 'Moses, Moses!' And he said, 'Here I am.' Then he said, 'Come no closer! Remove the sandals from your feet, for the place on which you are standing is holy ground.'

One of my favourite photographs of my daughter was taken when she was just a baby, at the local garden centre, where for a few minutes she lay in her pram gazing up at a fuchsia flower with totally rapt attention. She was seeing her first fuchsia. She could have been the very first person ever to see a fuchsia and be overwhelmed by the wonder and beauty of it. She was on holy ground, and somewhere in her infant heart she knew it.

When babies are caught up in a moment of wonder like this, nothing else exists for them. Their hearts and minds are still unburdened by all the baggage they will accumulate along life's way. Such moments are time-less, when there is no past to regret, no fear for the future. Moses has plenty to regret and even more to fear, yet his wonder overcomes everything as he stands in awe before the burning bush and knows that he stands on holy ground.

Contemplative prayer takes us to that eternal moment in the core of our being, when time stands still and our hearts are momentarily free of all the clutter, stilled into receptivity. Then we too can look into a flower and see eternity. We can walk through the park and see the blaze of glory in every bush.

May we know the wonder and joy of the timeless moments
that only the quietened, focused, contemplative heart can receive,
and only God can give.

MARGARET SILF

Connecting earth and heaven

Jacob left Beer-sheba and went towards Haran. He came to a certain place and stayed there for the night, because the sun had set. Taking one of the stones of the place, he put it under his head and lay down in that place. And he dreamed that there was a ladder set up on the earth, the top of it reaching to heaven; and the angels of God were ascending and descending on it... Then Jacob woke from his sleep and said, 'Surely the Lord is in this place – and I did not know it!'

Today we are given a little vignette from a hard and stony journey as Jacob makes his weary way towards Haran. Night falls. All he has is the rocky ground and a stone for a pillow – hardly the setting for calm contemplation. However, part of the secret of contemplation is to allow ourselves to be drawn into those layers of heart and soul that lie below the level of the conscious mind. Prayer can lead us there, as can music, poetry, the natural world and, of course, the gift of sleep. Ironically, it is in the darkness of sleep that Jacob finds the gift of enlightenment.

Our unconscious minds often communicate their wisdom through symbols. Jacob's ladder is a wonderful example. It also teaches us that authentic contemplative prayer can connect heaven and earth. It opens our hearts to recognise the many ways in which our daily lived experience, even at its hardest, can be suffused with the glory of God.

True contemplative prayer is not a withdrawal from everyday life, but a deeper immersion into it. It invites us to go deep within, to find God at the core of our being, and then to return to our everyday lives, bringing with us the heart knowledge that everything we do and everything we are has its source and its destiny in God. It takes us, for a timeless moment, to the top of the heavenly ladder, and then calls us to return to the place on earth and proclaim, with Jacob, that 'the Lord is in this place – and I did not know it!'

May we recognise the presence of God along the stony paths as well as in the consolations of prayer.

MARGARET SILF

Emptiness transformed

On the third day there was a wedding in Cana of Galilee, and the mother of Jesus was there. Jesus and his disciples had also been invited to the wedding. When the wine gave out… his mother said to the servants, 'Do whatever he tells you.' Now standing there were six stone water-jars for the Jewish rites of purification, each holding twenty or thirty gallons. Jesus said to them, 'Fill the jars with water.' And they filled them up to the brim. He said to them, 'Now draw some out and take it to the chief steward.'

The miracle at Cana could be a textbook exercise in the practice of contemplative prayer. We are all familiar with the story of Jesus' first miracle. The phrase 'turning water into wine' has become a cliché, used by many who have never read the original story.

This story of transformation, however, is also almost a step-by-step guide to contemplation. The first, most crucial stage of the process is emptiness. The wine has given out. Mary is the first to notice this and make Jesus aware of the crisis, and when the wine runs out in the middle of a wedding feast, there really is a crisis, at least at the human level.

Contemplative prayer also begins with emptiness, but because our minds are so constantly occupied with minor and major matters, we need to learn certain techniques for emptying them, for clearing out the clutter, perhaps by using a mantra or familiar phrase to still ourselves and, as it were, put our unruly thoughts aside, into a playpen, so that our hearts can focus on the desire to go deeper into God.

Into this situation of emptiness Jesus issues the call to fill up the vessels with the water needed for cleansing. We too are invited to come to stillness and allow the muddy waters of our minds to settle, leaving clear water in its place.

Only then can the transformation happen. The water at Cana becomes wine. The water of our daily lives is transformed through grace into the wine of a life lived in God.

May we have the grace to let ourselves be emptied out, the patience to await the settling of our souls and the joy of tasting the wine.

MARGARET SILF

A question of priorities

Now as they went on their way, he entered a certain village, where a woman named Martha welcomed him into her home. She had a sister named Mary, who sat at the Lord's feet and listened to what he was saying. But Martha was distracted by her many tasks; so she came to him and asked, 'Lord, do you not care that my sister has left me to do all the work by myself? Tell her then to help me.' But the Lord answered her, 'Martha, Martha, you are worried and distracted by many things; there is need of only one thing. Mary has chosen the better part, which will not be taken away from her.'

When I let my imagination rove over this story I see an exhausted Jesus, looking for a time of rest. Everyone wants a piece of him, and right now what he longs for is some peace and quiet. He has a bolthole with his dear friends in Bethany. They welcome him warmly as always, and Martha bustles around in the kitchen, preparing a meal for them. Mary meanwhile sits at Jesus' feet, and they share the quiet conversation of trusted friends.

I guess many readers feel a lot of sympathy with Martha. Hospitality, after all, is a sacred duty, and everyone wants a meal. So how do we feel about Jesus' apparent favouring of Mary in this situation? Perhaps it has something to tell us about the value of contemplation.

I wonder whether this story is less about favouring one sister's choice over that of the other but rather an invitation to reflect on our priorities. The meal is important, but there are some things that are even more important. We might almost hear Jesus murmuring quietly to Martha, as he draws her lovingly into his presence and invites her to sit beside her sister, 'Martha, first things first.'

There is a Martha and Mary in each of us. Our inner Martha does need to attend to the practical life, but our inner Mary also needs to sit quietly in the presence of God. Sometimes it is a matter of priorities.

There is a time for work and a time for prayer. May we learn to honour each in its right time.

MARGARET SILF

Non-transferable grace

'Ten bridesmaids took their lamps and went to meet the bridegroom. Five of them were foolish, and five were wise. When the foolish took their lamps, they took no oil with them; but the wise took flasks of oil with their lamps... At midnight there was a shout, "Look! Here is the bridegroom! Come out to meet him." Then all those bridesmaids got up and trimmed their lamps. The foolish said to the wise, "Give us some of your oil, for our lamps are going out." But the wise replied, "No! There will not be enough for you and for us; you had better go to the dealers and buy some for yourselves."'

I once heard someone say, 'When I miss prayer for a day, God notices. When I miss prayer for a week, I notice. When I miss prayer for a month, everyone notices.' The energy we tap into in contemplation makes a difference. We carry it with us through our day-to-day living, just as the wise bridesmaids carry the spare oil for their lamps. An hour's contemplation is a gift in itself, but it also supplies the spiritual energy for all the hours ahead, when daily life will make its heavy demands on us. We can walk through our day assured that our spiritual flasks are well topped-up.

What do we make of the refusal of the wise bridesmaids to share their oil with their less mindful sisters? Is it a bit mean-spirited? When we apply this story to the practice of contemplation, we see one very important thing: the energy and grace that is given in prayer is non-transferable. Each of us has to find our own pathway into prayer. Certainly the fruits of that prayer can and do nourish many more people than ourselves, because they change the way we relate to the world around us. The heart that is anchored in God through prayer will always bear fruit for many and in all seasons, like the tree planted by the water. But each of us is individually responsible for making our own journey to the well of contemplation.

May we have the grace to take responsibility for our own contemplative journey and then generously share its fruits with all those who have need of them.

MARGARET SILF

A place apart

'And whenever you pray, do not be like the hypocrites; for they love to stand and pray in the synagogues and at the street corners, so that they may be seen by others. Truly I tell you, they have received their reward. But whenever you pray, go into your room and shut the door and pray to your Father who is in secret; and your Father who sees in secret will reward you. When you are praying, do not heap up empty phrases as the Gentiles do; for they think that they will be heard because of their many words.'

On a busy flight from Glasgow to Dubai a quiet young woman with a boisterous toddler sat across the aisle from me. For the first two hours she tended the child patiently until he finally fell asleep, his head on her lap. I assumed she would now relax. Instead she turned towards the window and the black night beyond, her hands folded in prayer. Half an hour later, she turned back, ran her hand lovingly over the child's sleeping head and returned to reading her magazine.

It was a powerful lesson about going to a still place and shutting the door. At the time we were flying directly over war-torn Iraq. Her quiet contemplation hovered like a blessing over the killing fields beneath us.

Today, at the beginning of Lent, we might pause to ask ourselves where, in today's frenzied world, we find our own inner space to go to, closing the door for a while against the daily demands of life. I have a friend who lives in an overcrowded flat in a deprived urban area. Her inner room is the view from her window of a tree growing on a patch of waste ground. That tree, in all its seasons, is her focal point, her doorway into contemplation.

Ash Wednesday is a doorway into a special time of reflection. How might we begin our Lenten journey by stepping through that doorway into a daily quiet space, trusting that the Father who sees all that happens in the secrecy of our souls meets us wherever we turn in our search for the holy mystery?

As Lent begins, may we meet God each day in our heart's wordless silence.

MARGARET SILF

No instructions needed

He also said, 'The kingdom of God is as if someone would scatter seed on the ground, and would sleep and rise night and day, and the seed would sprout and grow, he does not know how. The earth produces of itself, first the stalk, then the head, then the full grain in the head. But when the grain is ripe, at once he goes in with his sickle, because the harvest has come.'

The simple act of sowing a seed is an act of faith. We drop a tiny speck of potential life into the cold earth, cover it up and let it disappear out of sight, and perhaps out of mind. The results may well surprise us as unexpected shoots and flowers emerge from that same cold earth a few months later.

To sow a seed, all that is needed is to tear open the seed packet and empty the contents into the ground. It would not occur to us to plant the seed packet along with the seed. The seed doesn't need any instructions about how and where it should be sown, how tall it will become or what it will look like when it blooms.

Contemplative prayer is a bit like that. It takes us into the depths of our being, where God is indwelling. We place ourselves into that stillness. The rest can safely be left to God. Our prayer doesn't need to give God any instructions as to how it should be answered. It doesn't need to include a wish list for all the blooms that we want our seed to produce.

Today's reading is a powerful reminder that prayer has an energy of its own. Time spent in stillness with God will sprout and grow in ways we do not understand and cannot necessarily see. It will flourish in its own way and its own time, without our help. We don't need to give it any instructions, nor should we dig it up to see how it is growing. Our only task is to gather the harvest in due season and share it with God's world.

May we learn to trust God more than we trust ourselves, as we sow our seeds of contemplation in the soil of God's infinite presence.

MARGARET SILF

In the eye of the storm

A gale swept down on the lake, and the boat was filling with water, and they were in danger. They went to him and woke him up, shouting, 'Master, Master, we are perishing!' And he woke up and rebuked the wind and the raging waves; they ceased, and there was a calm. He said to them, 'Where is your faith?' They were afraid and amazed, and said to one another, 'Who then is this, that he commands even the winds and the water, and they obey him?'

I once witnessed a disturbing scene involving a furious outburst by one person in a group of several friends. So fierce was the firestorm that erupted that several of the group immediately removed themselves from the scene. I could completely understand why they did so. They were genuinely afraid. The force of the negative energy flowing from the person who was causing the storm was like lava from an erupting volcano.

But one young woman stayed in the midst of the furore. She didn't say anything or enter the fray in any way. She simply stood there, eyes closed, in quiet prayer. While most people fled from the fury, she held herself, still and steady, in the eye of the hurricane.

The incident reminded me vividly of the story in today's reading. Jesus' friends are panicking, terrified for their lives and helpless to withstand the force of the storm. If they could have fled the onslaught of the waves they would surely have done so, but there is nowhere to go. So they turn to Jesus in their distress.

Jesus, asleep in the boat, is actually the still point at the eye of the storm. Perhaps there is a lesson for us here about the power of contemplative prayer. It takes a special kind of courage to stand our ground in calm and quiet when the storms of life are swirling dangerously all around us. This story assures us that this still point is the only place from which real and lasting peace can ultimately flow. Our world needs this peace today as desperately as those on that beleaguered little boat in Galilee.

In contemplation may we discover that the stillness
is more powerful than the storm.

MARGARET SILF

Awake at sunrise

'Be dressed for action and have your lamps lit; be like those who are waiting for their master to return from the wedding banquet, so that they may open the door for him as soon as he comes and knocks. Blessed are those slaves whom the master finds alert when he comes; truly I tell you, he will fasten his belt and have them sit down to eat, and he will come and serve them. If he comes during the middle of the night, or near dawn, and finds them so, blessed are those slaves.'

A story is told of a spiritual guru who taught his followers various spiritual practices and methods of prayer and meditation. They in turn spent much time trying to put into practice the techniques they were learning from him. One day one of the students asked the guru, 'What can I do to achieve enlightenment?' The guru replied with another question, 'What can you do to make the sun rise?' The student, taken off guard by this unexpected response, admitted, 'There is nothing I can do to make the sun rise.' The guru smiled, 'And there is nothing you can do to achieve enlightenment.' Frustrated now, the student asked, a touch querulously, 'So why are you asking us to practise all these meditation techniques?' 'So that you will be awake when the sun rises,' replied the guru.

There are many different ways of practising prayer and contemplation. There is no one 'right' way, and no practice, if truly rooted in God, is 'wrong'. None of them delivers a finished product called 'enlightenment'. Each of them offers a particular way of preparing our hearts to recognise the glimpses of the divine presence when we encounter it, and to live in its light even when we don't see it.

We too, like the guru's students, can become so eager to grasp a light that still lies beyond the horizon of our understanding that we fail to engage with the daily disciplines that are preparing us to recognise the light when it dawns; so concerned with achieving 'nirvana' that we seek to bypass the practices that help us watch and wait for the master's coming.

We are not called to achieve anything, but to stay awake, hearts and minds prepared, receptive and alert, to welcome the dawning of God's new day.

MARGARET SILF

Place

Places are important to us as human beings for many reasons. There are places we have left and never wish to revisit, and there are places that are held dear in our heart even if we are now far removed from them. As embodied beings, we are confined to space and time and therefore places have meaning for us, for we are earthed in this world.

Throughout scripture God meets with people in different places, some of them already loaded with significance because of something that happened there. Thus Jerusalem, the holy city, was special to the Jewish nation as the place where God had his dwelling, the temple. This example is a reminder, however, of the ephemeral nature of places, for the time came when God's people were taken away into exile and the temple was destroyed. The people had to learn how to sing the Lord's song in a strange land, a place where God's name was not honoured. Most of the exiles did not expect him to show up there and had to learn that God is not confined to space and time and is present everywhere, waiting to come to all those who seek him.

Today we can theoretically go anywhere we please. In the west, at least, we have a mobile society, always on the move, restless and seeking new thrills in new places. Yet God is here, now, in the very places we find ourselves at this moment. What is more, he longs to make himself known. 'The word is very near to you; it is in your mouth and in your heart' (Deuteronomy 30:14, NRSV). The readings for the next two weeks explore how people met with God in different places. They frequently bear out the truth of the poet R.S. Thomas' words: 'You gave me only this small pool that the more I drink from, the more overflows me with sourceless light' ('The Gift'). They invite us to see with fresh eyes the places we have visited in the past and currently inhabit and say with Jacob at Bethel, 'Surely the Lord is in this place... This is none other than the house of God, and this is the gate of heaven' (Genesis 28:16–17, NRSV).

LIZ HOARE

The altar: the place where it began

[Abram] journeyed on by stages from the Negeb as far as Bethel, to the place where his tent had been at the beginning, between Bethel and Ai, to the place where he had made an altar at the first; and there Abram called on the name of the Lord.

It may seem strange to begin a series of Bible notes on 'place' with a wandering nomad retracing his steps, but Abram's return to the location where he first called on the name of the Lord was a vital reference point in his spiritual development. It was the place he had pitched his tent and built an altar, actions that marked the spot as significant for a physical and spiritual journey combined. The tent was packed away for the next phase of the journey, but that pile of stones remained as a sign that here Abram had communed with God.

The letter to the Hebrews tells us that when God first called Abram (Genesis 12:1), he set out 'not knowing where he was going' (Hebrews 11:8). This may sound irresponsible, especially to people who are used to travelling with a map and a destination, complete with good places to stop for rest and refuelling, but Abram was learning to walk by faith and not by sight (2 Corinthians 5:7). His directions consisted of a promise from God that he would be shown a land full of blessing. So he, along with his family and possessions, journeyed from place to place, learning along the way.

Abram's walk of faith was not straightforward, however, and things went wrong in Egypt. How could Abram recover from this disastrous turn of events? Wisely, he went back to where he had heard God clearly and first found his bearings. Abram needed them, for almost immediately he faced a new challenge with his nephew Lot, but this time he acted with wisdom and discretion. The place where he had made an altar to the Lord became for Abram the place of regeneration and transformation.

Thank you, Lord, for the anchor points in my walk with you.
Help me to recall them in times of darkness. Amen

LIZ HOARE

Peniel: the place of wrestling

Jacob was left alone; and a man wrestled with him until daybreak. When the man saw that he did not prevail against Jacob, he struck him on the hip socket; and Jacob's hip was put out of joint as he wrestled with him. Then he said, 'Let me go, for the day is breaking.' But Jacob said, 'I will not let you go, unless you bless me.' So he said to him, 'What is your name?' And he said 'Jacob.' Then the man said, 'You shall no longer be called Jacob, but Israel, for you have striven with God and with humans, and have prevailed.'

I can recall walking down the lane close to where we lived in the darkness, shouting aloud to God about my situation. It is the closest I have come to a felt experience of wrestling with God and emerging from that place changed in the depths of my heart. I will never forget the physical darkness that seemed to mirror my own interior confusion, and the experience is forever linked to that physical place.

Once before Jacob had marked a physical spot as the place of encounter with God – when he set up a stone at Bethel (Genesis 28:18). Now he was himself marked with a physical reminder of a further encounter with God. His limp would be the permanent mark of what happened at the ford of Jabbok. It was here that he made preparations to meet his brother and finally face the music of a lifetime of manipulation and deceit. Would he ever change? It took a physical wrestling match and a battle of wills before he found redemption. But when the sun came up, he crossed the ford as a changed man. The water of the river and the before and after experience are akin to a baptism, signifying a crossing place, from the death of the old to something new. As with baptism, Jacob received his name, and would be the namesake of God's people – Israel.

Lord, help me to find the courage to persevere in prayer and to allow you to mould my heart and soul so that I am changed. Amen

LIZ HOARE

The burning bush: the place of encounter with compassion

Moses… led his flock beyond the wilderness and came to Horeb, the mountain of God. There the angel of the Lord appeared to him in a flame of fire out of a bush… Then the Lord said, 'I have observed the misery of my people who are in Egypt; I have heard their cry on account of their taskmasters. Indeed, I know their sufferings, and I have come down to deliver them…'

Like Jacob's encounter at the ford, this appearance of God to a human being in the Old Testament is called a theophany. Such a phenomenon is never God simply playing games. His appearing is always accompanied by words, and it is the message they contain that is all-important. Here Moses was shepherding his flock in a familiar place when he noticed something unusual: a bush that was aflame but not burned up. He paused to look more closely and, having got Moses' attention, God spoke to him. He revealed himself as the God of compassion who had heard his people's cry and was coming to deliver them.

Many people attest to having had an extraordinary experience they cannot explain. For some it leads to an encounter with the living God, as it did that day for Moses. An ordinary bush turned into an extraordinary encounter that revealed the character of God and instigated a call to action on Moses' part. Moses could not make this happen, and indeed at first he would rather it had not, for it was to make life-changing demands. We cannot engineer God's coming, but we can learn to pay attention so that we are attuned to the eternal in the present.

Today, as part of your prayers, think through the day ahead and ask the Lord to meet you in the ordinary places of work, home, journeying, meetings and rest. Learning to have eyes to see and ears to hear will mean also having hearts that are open to being changed as a result of seeing and hearing and responding in obedience.

Lord, may I meet you in the ordinary places and respond to your call today.
Amen

LIZ HOARE

The wilderness: the place of formation

He sustained him in a desert land, in a howling wilderness waste; he shielded him, cared for him, guarded him as the apple of his eye. As an eagle stirs up its nest, and hovers over its young; as it spreads its wings, takes them up, and bears them aloft on its pinions, the Lord alone guided him.

Wildernesses are generally unpromising places. As here, words like 'howling waste', or 'barren', 'wild', 'dry' and 'unproductive' come to mind. What good could possibly occur in such a place? Perhaps you are experiencing a wilderness in your life right now. It may not be physical, but your job, home life or even place of worship just feels barren and harsh. Today's reading is part of the so-called Song of Moses, a hymn of praise to the faithfulness of the Lord God followed by the recounting of Israel's failure to respond in a like manner and returning to God's compassion and mercy in the latter verses (Deuteronomy 32:1–43). We can see that the wilderness is the place where God shaped his people, and the landscape itself had an important part to play. In the wilderness the people were vulnerable; they had to learn to depend on God for safety and protection, as when he accompanied them in a pillar of cloud by day and fire by night. They had to rely on him for sustenance and received manna and water from the rock. They had to learn the difficult art of waiting while Moses was on the mountain with God and they experienced the stripping away of all the former things that had made their lives tolerable in Egypt. Over and over again they failed, but God remained faithful.

Today's reading offers two beautiful images of God's ways with us: we are the apple of his eye, precious beyond telling, and he watches over us like a mother eagle guarding her young. The eagle's purpose is to see her young fly and become mature eagles themselves, just as God's ways with us are forming us into the likeness of Christ, even in our wilderness places.

Lord Jesus, sustain me in my wilderness places and watch over me. Amen

LIZ HOARE

The Jordan River: the place of remembering

'Pass on before the ark of the Lord your God into the middle of the Jordan, and each of you take up a stone on his shoulder, one for each of the tribes of the Israelites, so that this may be a sign among you. When your children ask in time to come, "What do these stones mean to you?" then you shall tell them that the waters of the Jordan were cut off in front of the ark of the covenant of the Lord… So these stones shall be to the Israelites a memorial for ever.'

Places bring back memories, and collective memories are often preserved by erecting a memorial of some kind. Many standing stones are so ancient that we do not know why they are there, but they seem to represent the significance of their resting place for the people who erected them. Later, early Christians of the British Isles put up great stone crosses inscribed with images from the Christian story. They made a statement about the victory of Christ on the cross, proclaiming that Jesus was Lord. I like to imagine people telling the stories recorded on the crosses and bearing witness to the good news of the gospel. These stones in the landscape 'spoke' powerfully of God's presence and character to all who saw them, but moreover they were a prompt to believers to pass on the message to others. God had acted as he had promised and sent a saviour.

Today's passage shows that same saving God at work to lead his people into the promised land. Having crossed the river, Joshua erected the twelve stones that the representative from each tribe had carried over as a memorial to what took place there. God had warned his people of the danger of forgetting his mighty acts of protection, provision and continuing presence once they had entered their new land (Deuteronomy 8). The stones were a reminder both of his strength and of the importance of remembering.

Thank you, Lord, for the memory stones in the story of your people. May they give hope to those in places where the future looks bleak today. Amen

LIZ HOARE

Elijah on Horeb: the place of recommissioning

[God] said, 'Go out and stand on the mountain before the Lord, for the Lord is about to pass by.' Now there was a great wind... but the Lord was not in the wind; and after the wind an earthquake, but the Lord was not in the earthquake; and after the earthquake a fire, but the Lord was not in the fire; and after the fire, a sound of sheer silence... Then there came a voice to him that said, 'What are you doing here, Elijah?'

Elijah went back the way he came, but not before he hit the depths of despair. Immediately after his great triumph on Mt Carmel and in terror of Queen Jezebel, he experienced a rollercoaster of emotions, from the heights to the depths. Having wished to die, he was sustained by the angel of the Lord in a practical way and came to a place where others before him had met with God. The place was deeply significant, but upon arriving there Elijah crept into a cave and went to sleep (v. 9). He was not yet ready to hear the Lord God speak to him. Like Moses, he witnessed natural phenomena that startled and amazed him. It was the 'sound of sheer silence' that finally summoned him to the entrance of his cave of abandonment to hear the restorative words of his Lord and master. Cowering under his mantle, he faced God's repeated question, and each time Elijah poured forth a catalogue of woe and abandonment. Then God reassured him that he was not alone and there were others to support him. It was with this reassurance that the Lord sent him back the way he had come to complete what he had begun.

Perhaps we have felt some of the emotions that Elijah experienced in his ministry: exhaustion, abandonment, failure, depression and despair. With such feelings, the future looks bleak and it's hard to find strength to go on. The place of recommissioning can be anywhere, but we too may have to allow the storm to rage within and without before we can let go and embrace God's ever-flowing compassion.

Lord, help me to listen to that still small voice today. Amen

LIZ HOARE

Isaiah in the temple: the place of healing

In the year that King Uzziah died, I saw the Lord sitting on a throne, high and lofty; and the hem of his robe filled the temple. Seraphs were in attendance above him... And one called to another and said: 'Holy, holy, holy is the Lord of hosts; the whole earth is full of his glory.'... And I said: 'Woe is me! I am lost, for I am a man of unclean lips... yet my eyes have seen the King, the Lord of hosts!' Then one of the seraphs flew to me, holding a live coal that had been taken from the altar with a pair of tongs. The seraph touched my mouth with it and said: 'Now that this has touched your lips, your guilt has departed and your sin is blotted out.' Then I heard the voice of the Lord saying, 'Whom shall I send, and who will go for us?' And I said, 'Here am I; send me!'

The power of Isaiah's vision is almost palpable. God's holiness overwhelms him, and he is stricken by his unworthiness. The vision in the temple could have been the place of destruction for him, for no one can see God and live (Exodus 33:20). Instead it became the place of healing. Fire in the Old Testament denotes the presence of the holy God. Taken directly from the altar, the holiest place, the coal's searing glow burns Isaiah's lips. God's holiness 'infects' Isaiah so that his sin is blotted out. 'Salvation' is a word that includes forgiveness of sins but also complete wholeness. It is all-encompassing: all the wounds, defects and deficiencies that we experience in this life are mended so that we become whole again.

Isaiah experienced God's amazing grace: 'I once was lost, but now am found, was blind, but now I see' (John Newton, 'Amazing Grace'). His restored condition made him ready and prepared to respond to God's call to go, whatever that might entail. God saves us not so that we may escape this world, but so that we may live the lives God intended for us here and now.

Lord, help me to enter more fully into your healing power today. Amen

LIZ HOARE

Nazareth: the place of obscurity

When they had finished everything required by the law of the Lord, they returned to Galilee, to their own town of Nazareth. The child grew and became strong, filled with wisdom; and the favour of God was upon him.

If we were planning the salvation of the world, most of us would choose auspicious beginnings, providing every resource known to humanity. God, however, persists in making unlikely choices, none more so than the circumstances of the incarnation. An occupied nation, a young girl with no prospects, a birth in squalor and, here in today's reading, an obscure town for the upbringing of his beloved son. Jesus spent the longest part of his life in Nazareth, and we are not even told what he did with all those years. We make our guesses: following in his father's footsteps as a carpenter perhaps; learning the faith of his ancestors surely, for he knew the scriptures as well as anyone. But why did God arrange things like this?

Today's world seems more complex than the age in which Jesus was born. But we know that, although knowledge has increased, wisdom is a different thing. Many people would like to be wise, but do not devote their lives to acquiring wisdom, for there is so much else to do. It seems that Jesus had a different set of priorities. 'He grew and became strong' suggests not just physical prowess but also strength of character. This goes hand in hand with becoming wise, and Luke reports that Jesus was 'filled' with wisdom.

How did he achieve this? Perhaps 'achieve' gives the wrong impression, for wisdom is not acquired by striving. It grows secretly as we attend to the important things. Luke's final comment is the clue: 'the favour of God was upon him'. He spent time with his heavenly Father, so much so that later he told people that he never did anything on his own, but only what he saw his Father doing (John 5:19). To be so in tune with God is to have gained wisdom of a kind that is beyond any price we could imagine.

Dear Lord, show me how to grow in wisdom. Amen

LIZ HOARE

Galilee: the place of calling

As Jesus passed along the Sea of Galilee, he saw Simon and his brother Andrew casting a net into the lake – for they were fishermen. And Jesus said to them, 'Follow me and I will make you fish for people.' And immediately they left their nets and followed him. As he went a little farther, he saw James son of Zebedee and his brother John, who were in their boat mending the nets. Immediately he called them; and they left their father Zebedee in the boat with the hired men, and followed him.

You may be one of those people who can recall exactly when and where you first responded to the gospel and became a follower of Jesus. Lent is a good time to pause to remember that first call: what it meant then and what it has meant since. It may have involved leaving behind a whole way of life, even family and friends, in order to follow where Jesus was calling you. For all of us, including those whose lives have evolved from a gradual seed of faith planted long ago, reminding ourselves of our call to follow and what it means is important.

We are called to be those who fish for people. That may involve direct evangelism. It will certainly mean that we travel through life as ambassadors for Christ, his call embedded in our DNA. Becoming a follower of Jesus will mean laying down certain things: ambitions, relationships, lifestyles and anything that threatens to encumber us in serving our new master. We are learning to march to a different drum. Simon, Andrew, James and John retained certain things from their old lives too: their names, the skills they had learned as fishermen (now put to new use) and their humanity.

Being called to follow Jesus involves finding out our true worth and purpose as human beings. At one point, Simon and some of the others returned to fishing for a short while, but it did not last. Their vision renewed, they set out again to follow in the footsteps of their master and Lord.

Lord, help me to love myself with open eyes,
so that I may more truly love you. Amen

LIZ HOARE

The well at Sychar: the place of insight

But [Jesus] had to go through Samaria. So he came to a Samaritan city called Sychar, near the plot of ground that Jacob had given to his son Joseph. Jacob's well was there, and Jesus, tired out by his journey, was sitting by the well. It was about noon. A Samaritan woman came to draw water, and Jesus said to her, 'Give me a drink.'

Did Jesus know that a disreputable woman would arrive with her water jar as he sat in the heat and dust of noonday? The story unfolds with a conversation that includes humour, challenge, question and answer, red herrings and more. The well at Sychar was a good place to gather for some conversation, especially for the women of the village drawing water for their daily needs, but Jesus was not there just for the idle chatter. He turned a simple request into a dialogue that was about life in all its fullness.

Later in his gospel, John describes Jesus crying out, 'Let anyone who is thirsty come to me, and let the one who believes in me drink. As the scripture has said, "Out of the believer's heart shall flow rivers of living water"' (John 7:37–38). It is a commentary on what happened as the woman moved from defensiveness about her past to curiosity about Jesus and then to realising that she was speaking to someone who could fulfil her deepest longings.

What is it that we long for? Sometimes the business of keeping up appearances or even just keeping going obscures our deepest needs so that we are unable to see what God is offering us. We think we have to do something dramatic to find release, or peace, or whatever it is we desire, but it is here in the midst of it all, if we could but see. The woman stayed at the well because she was intrigued and then captivated by Jesus. She had the privilege of his sitting in front of her. We too may come close and hear him speaking into our lives, so that we gain the insight needed to quench our thirst with the water of life.

Lord Jesus, give me to drink from the well of salvation today. Amen

LIZ HOARE

The mountain: the place of transfiguration

Six days later, Jesus took with him Peter and James and John, and led them up a high mountain apart, by themselves. And he was transfigured before them, and his clothes became dazzling white, such as no one on earth could bleach them. And there appeared to them Elijah with Moses, who were talking with Jesus. Then Peter said to Jesus, 'Rabbi, it is good for us to be here; let us make three dwellings, one for you, one for Moses, and one for Elijah.' He did not know what to say, for they were terrified. Then a cloud overshadowed them, and from the cloud there came a voice, 'This is my Son, the Beloved; listen to him!'

In this extraordinary event, Peter, James and John saw and heard things far beyond their human experience to date. It is no wonder they were terrified! Peter is often castigated for his exclamation, but he may have been more aware than we think of what was taking place and have wanted simply to honour the divinity that was present. Whatever he thought at the time, he came to realise that he had been with God on the mountain and had witnessed a whole other reality. He saw something of God's glory. God's glory was revealed and for a moment the disciples were caught up into God's eternity. This was to have a lasting effect on Peter and how he understood Jesus (cf. 2 Peter 1:16–18). It is a reminder that in Christ, heaven has come close and there is so much more to be revealed.

Every place has the potential to be the place where God's glory may be glimpsed in ways that transfigure the situation and enable us to see it from God's eternal perspective. Above all, we are challenged, like the disciples, to listen to God's son, Jesus, and obey. The Latin word for 'obey' contains the meaning 'to listen'. The two actions are closely linked. God's transfiguring presence invites us to be part of the change that is needed.

Lord, help me to listen to Jesus, the Lord of glory, and learn to see things from your perspective. Amen

LIZ HOARE

The home of Mary, Martha and Lazarus: the place of friendship

Now a certain man was ill, Lazarus of Bethany, the village of Mary and her sister Martha. Mary was the one who anointed the Lord with perfume and wiped his feet with her hair; her brother Lazarus was ill. So the sisters sent a message to Jesus, 'Lord, he whom you love is ill.'

These few verses tell us a great deal about the home at Bethany and Jesus' relationship with it and its occupants. Bethany was a small village outside Jerusalem frequented by Jesus, who found refuge and friendship there. Mary, Martha and Lazarus seem to have been as family to him, and perhaps it was one of the few places where he could relax and enjoy company over food and conversation. It is a reminder of the human side of Jesus, a reminder that the incarnation involved the Word's becoming flesh and blood. If we downplay this, we risk inventing a Jesus who cannot share our humanity at any level.

As today's reading unfolds, we witness the humanity of Jesus in vivid detail as he weeps over the death of his dear friend. 'Surely he has borne our griefs' (Isaiah 53:4, ESV)? But the home at Bethany is a place where Jesus' divinity is touched on also. Key events took place there and John reminds us of one of them: the anointing of Jesus' feet by Mary shortly before his crucifixion (see John 12:1–8). This was a prophetic act on her part, which Jesus regarded as preparation for his death. Mary's costly and extravagant gesture was one of deep love, poured out for him as he would pour out his life for her and for all of us in his death.

Clearly this little family loved Jesus, and their mutual vulnerability had built trust and a depth of friendship that was Mary and Martha's strongest hope in a time of crisis. At this stage Jesus was their brother's only hope. Jesus did not need their bold reminder that Lazarus was beloved, but then as now he delights to hear our words of love and devotion.

Lord Jesus, thank you that you call us friends.
Help me to grow in friendship with you. Amen

LIZ HOARE

Gethsemane: the place of struggle

They went to a place called Gethsemane; and [Jesus] said to his disciples, 'Sit here while I pray.' He took with him Peter and James and John, and began to be distressed and agitated. And he said to them, 'I am deeply grieved, even to death; remain here, and keep awake.' And going a little farther, he threw himself on the ground and prayed that, if it were possible, the hour might pass from him. He said, 'Abba, Father, for you all things are possible; remove this cup from me; yet, not what I want, but what you want.'

Gethsemane was a favourite location of Jesus, who often met there with his disciples (see John 18:2). It was a garden of olive trees on the slope of the Mount of Olives, and the name literally means 'olive press.' All four gospels describe events there just before Jesus' crucifixion, and it was a place of enormous significance for Jesus. Jesus knew that the great crisis of his earthly life was approaching, so he went to a place where he could pray. He also wanted company in his hour of need, so he took with him his closest disciples. He asked them to keep vigil, but the struggle was his alone. Wrestling in prayer, he faced the future with dread, even as he sought the presence of his heavenly Father.

We may have witnessed someone struggling with what lies ahead and seen how body, mind and spirit are all caught up in agony. Jesus was 'distressed' and 'agitated' and the word he used of himself was 'grieved'. These are all characteristics of someone undergoing a great struggle. Does it shock us that Jesus shrank from his ordeal and sought release 'if possible'? The scene records a battle of cosmic proportions going on and Jesus at the heart of it. Yet to the end he desired to align his will with the Father. In our own struggles, it is not a cop-out to echo Jesus' prayer, for prayer is above all about aligning our wills with the will of the Lord of the universe, who works all things together for good.

Not my will but yours be done, dear Lord. Amen

LIZ HOARE

Calvary: the place of remembrance

One of the criminals who were hanged there kept deriding him and saying, 'Are you not the Messiah? Save yourself and us.' But the other rebuked him, saying, 'Do you not fear God…?' Then he said, 'Jesus, remember me when you come into your kingdom.' He replied, 'Truly I tell you, today you will be with me in Paradise.' It was now about noon, and darkness came over the whole land until three in the afternoon, while the sun's light failed; and the curtain of the temple was torn in two. Then Jesus, crying with a loud voice, said, 'Father, into your hands I commend my spirit.' Having said this, he breathed his last.

The fear of being forgotten is a deeply held human trait and one of the main reasons why death is so threatening. Who will remember us when we're gone? The second criminal had it right when he asked Jesus to remember him. The irony of the first criminal's words is striking when placed alongside Jesus' response to the plea of the second. Jesus was indeed the Messiah, but his kingdom is not of this world, though it is being established even now in this world and one day will be complete. Believers inhabit both realms, and salvation crosses the divide. The two sayings from the cross recorded here show Jesus first of all reassuring the second criminal that he would remember him, while his words to his heavenly Father show the trust he had that God would not abandon or forget his beloved son. Placed alongside his words in John, 'It is finished' (John 19:30), Jesus' act of relinquishment of his life and breath is done with confidence that God will remember his commitment to him and receive him in glory.

We can pray this prayer in trust each day as we lie down to sleep, and it holds true for us as we draw our final breath also. God is faithful, and he will remember us. After all, he knows us by name, we are his, because of the battle that Jesus won on the cross.

Jesus, remember me when you come into your kingdom. Amen

LIZ HOARE

Exile

In recent years we have become all too familiar with tragic tales of exile. From the safety of our homes, we have witnessed on our screens the plight of those who, forced to flee their homeland because of poverty or violence, find themselves crushed into fragile boats as they make desperate journeys to new lands. These lands will inevitably be for them places of exile. Some of them may be acquainted with the biblical stories of the exile. Lamentations, several of the psalms and the cries of the exilic prophets will resonate deeply with their experience, offering comfort in the companionship of those ancient people who not only survived in exile but also found the precious gift of hope.

But this expulsion from a beloved homeland is not the only form of exile. Exile is where you find yourself feeling not at home: the place that seems unfamiliar, where you are deprived of those home comforts that normally make you feel safe in this world. The moment we are born we experience exile, as we are evicted from the safe haven of the womb. From that moment on we can experience all kinds of exiles as we journey through life: starting a new school, moving to a new town, losing the safety and familiarity of a significant friendship, working in an environment that feels hostile, living in a world that feels alien because of illness or injury, and many others. Though many of these may not have the terrible severity of being uprooted from your homeland, nevertheless they can feel hugely disturbing. Lent can be a form of voluntary exile – where we choose to deprive ourselves of something that would normally be one of the comforts of home.

As we explore the scriptures, we see many stories of humans like ourselves who found themselves in an exile situation and who looked to God for help. And what we find is that exile can be full of possibility and wonder. It can also be a place of discovering the presence of God in surprising ways. In the next two weeks we shall look at some of these stories and draw inspiration from them for the times when life takes us into experiences of exile.

MICHAEL MITTON

Exile from Eden

Then the Lord God said, 'See, the man has become like one of us, knowing good and evil; and now, he might reach out his hand and take also from the tree of life, and eat, and live for ever' – therefore the Lord God sent him forth from the garden of Eden, to till the ground from which he was taken. He drove out the man; and at the east of the garden of Eden he placed the cherubim, and a sword flaming and turning to guard the way to the tree of life.

The first two chapters of the Bible describe a place and tell a story. The place is a garden that is the most special of all gardens. It is a place unspoilt by any kind of damage. The story is about the creation of two human beings who inhabit this beautiful place perfectly. They are in harmony with each other and with God. Nothing tarnishes this wonderful world, until we get to chapter 3, and then it feels as if all hell breaks loose, and in many senses it does. It is almost unbearable to read of the terrible decisions the humans take as they imagine that there is even greener grass on the other side of this perfect world. As a consequence of their decision, they are exiled from this garden, and the rest of the Bible is about humans trying to find their way back.

It is good to return to this story from time to time, not to analyse it but to dwell in it – to read the first chapters and connect with our own longing for this unspoilt paradise, and then to feel the sense of loss as we depart with Adam and Eve to the land beyond that flaming sword. We realise it is not their story, but our story. However comfortable or safe we may feel in this world, there is always that nagging doubt that things could be better. Lent is an excellent time for listening to this yearning. Such a yearning properly disturbs our settledness and stirs us to pray 'your kingdom come… on earth as it is in heaven' (Matthew 6:10) – and to work for it.

Lord, may your kingdom come in this world, as it is in paradise.

MICHAEL MITTON

Lament in exile

How lonely sits the city that once was full of people! How like a widow she has become, she that was great among the nations! She that was a princess among the provinces has become a vassal. She weeps bitterly in the night, with tears on her cheeks; among all her lovers she has no one to comfort her; all her friends have dealt treacherously with her, they have become her enemies. Judah has gone into exile with suffering and hard servitude…

The destruction of Jerusalem by Nebuchadnezzar in 587BC, and the enforced exile in Babylon of many of its citizens, was a horrendous calamity for the people of God. The impossible had happened, and the result was death, starvation, destruction and exile. Those traumatised people who found themselves as captives in a foreign land needed words to give expression to the overwhelming sense of devastation and loss they had experienced. The book of Lamentations is an attempt to provide such words.

If you are well and content, the words of this book will probably just seem depressing. However, if you find yourself in any kind of exile, this book is a remarkable gift. It is written by one who has managed to find words to express their emotional jumble of grief, failure, guilt, fear and rage. They say it as it is. What is wonderful is that they feel they can do this safely in the presence of God, because they have discovered that God is one who listens compassionately to human suffering. Yes, in their case, their exile was partly of their own making, and there is penitence in these lamentations. But more than anything, this book gives permission to any of us to express our hurt and suffering to God, and to know that such laments are held in the heart of heaven.

And set right in the middle of the book is an astonishing cry of hope, because lamenting in the presence of God opens our hearts to perceiving his compassion and love: 'But this I call to mind, and therefore I have hope: The steadfast love of the Lord never ceases, his mercies never come to an end' (Lamentations 3:21–22).

Compassionate God, thank you for hearing my laments.

MICHAEL MITTON

Memory in exile

Listen to me, you that pursue righteousness, you that seek the Lord. Look to the rock from which you were hewn, and to the quarry from which you were dug. Look to Abraham your father and to Sarah who bore you; for he was but one when I called him, but I blessed him and made him many. For the Lord will comfort Zion; he will comfort all her waste places, and will make her wilderness like Eden, her desert like the garden of the Lord...

The second part of the book of Isaiah is often called 'the book of comfort' and is addressed to exiles. It begins with the famous 'Comfort my people' exhortation in chapter 40, and it includes the references to the servant of God, who not only comforts the people but also suffers with them. In the midst of this section comes the wonderful promise that God will not only comfort broken Zion but will also transform its wilderness, that it might flourish like the garden of Eden. The passage evokes that yearning for Eden again. And how is this hope engaged? The prophet says that the path is found by the act of remembering.

Remembering is a key discipline for exiles. But it is a particular type of remembering. It is not a harking back to the good old days or a wallowing in nostalgia. It is a remembering that empowers for the future. In the case of today's passage, the exiles are invited to remember Abraham and Sarah, to recall their faith and the fact that God worked such wonders through them. If God brought such abundance of generations from a couple who were apparently past their childbearing years, then he can breathe life back into listless exiles. Such remembering kindles energising hope.

When we find ourselves in an exile situation, it is a helpful discipline to look back at the ways God has led us in the past. Lent is an excellent time for looking back and retelling for ourselves and others how God has worked in us. Such remembering can open us to new possibilities of faith.

Breathe on my memories, Holy Spirit, that my remembering may lead me to discover the gardens of the Lord.

MICHAEL MITTON

Presence in exile

In the thirtieth year, in the fourth month, on the fifth day of the month, as I was among the exiles by the river Chebar, the heavens were opened, and I saw visions of God. On the fifth day of the month (it was the fifth year of the exile of King Jehoiachin), the word of the Lord came to the priest Ezekiel son of Buzi, in the land of the Chaldeans by the river Chebar; and the hand of the Lord was on him there.

One of the people uprooted from Jerusalem and hauled into exile was a young priest called Ezekiel. The traditional belief was that God gave his people a specific land – the land of Israel – and at the centre of this land was the great city of Zion, which was the city of God. And the place where God dwelt most directly was in the temple built by the great King Solomon. Knock down the temple and destroy the city and utter chaos would ensue, for where would God abide? The people of Israel who were marched into captivity in Babylon were faced not only with a terrible social crisis but a theological one as well. As they saw it, God had effectively been evicted from his land. How could they possibly ever make contact with him again?

Well, it seems that Ezekiel was open to a development of this theology. Perhaps it surprised him as much as anyone else that while he was dwelling in the very place of desolation he saw visions of God. Jerusalem was closed for business, but heaven was open. From that moment Ezekiel became a remarkable seer, witnessing visions that have intrigued, baffled and delighted people ever since. These visions proved one thing clearly – God was not confining his presence to just one place and one temple. His presence was available even in exile.

Exile brings disturbance. We may feel deprived of the usual routines that help us connect with God. Ezekiel would tell us that this is the ideal setting for gaining new visions of God. Any place can be the starting point for gaining a new vision of God.

Lord God, give me the eyes to behold visions of you.

MICHAEL MITTON

Hope in exile

Then he said to me, 'Prophesy to the breath, prophesy, mortal, and say to the breath: Thus says the Lord God: Come from the four winds, O breath, and breathe upon these slain, that they may live.' I prophesied as he commanded me, and the breath came into them, and they lived, and stood on their feet, a vast multitude. Then he said to me, 'Mortal, these bones are the whole house of Israel. They say, "Our bones are dried up, and our hope is lost; we are cut off completely."'

We stay with Ezekiel for another day. He is a prophet specifically called by God to work with people in exile. His task is to lift them from a rather parochial view of God to something much bigger. There is much in the first part of his book that is about judgement on the people of God for their infidelity, and those listening to this prophet would be in no doubt that they had been the cause of their own downfall. Then from chapter 33 we start hearing messages of hope. The people have to acknowledge the bad news before they can fully appreciate the good news.

The message of hope is none other than the message of resurrection. The vision of the valley of dry bones is effectively saying that the exiles don't amount to anything more than a pile of dead bones. All hope is lost. However, there is one thing that can change all of this – the breath of God. The God of the impossible can transform the bones of death into an army of life. The breath of God creates a new future. And how does the breath come? It is summoned by the prophet.

Another discipline of exile is the inbreathing of new life. In Christ, we too can engage prophetically in the great act of invoking the Holy Spirit of God to quicken that which has apparently died. Ezekiel would encourage us to recognise that the moment when our normal securities are removed may be the very time to summon the breath of God. Even in Lent we are a resurrection people.

---

*If you are aware of an apparently lifeless situation today,
call on the breath of God for new life.*

MICHAEL MITTON

Love in exile

So [Naomi] said, 'See, your sister-in-law has gone back to her people and to her gods; return after your sister-in-law.' But Ruth said, 'Do not press me to leave you or to turn back from following you! Where you go, I will go; where you lodge, I will lodge; your people shall be my people, and your God my God. Where you die, I will die – there will I be buried.'

One of the most tragic stories of exile comes in the book of Ruth. It begins with Naomi. She, her husband and sons are forced into exile because of famine. They flee to Moab, a one-time enemy of Israel's. There the two sons marry Moabite women, but Naomi's husband and two sons die. A more tragic scene is hard to imagine. Naomi decides she must return to her homeland. Her daughter-in-law, Ruth, decides to opt for voluntary exile because of the great love she has developed for Naomi. Today's reading is a remarkable declaration of love and commitment to someone not only of a different nationality, but from a nation that has been an enemy.

Thus Ruth and Naomi make their way to Bethlehem. Ruth is now a widow in exile and is very vulnerable. Naomi is back home, and yet her severely bereaved soul is still in exile; she exclaims, 'the Almighty has dealt bitterly with me' (v. 20). Ruth, however, seems to harbour no bitterness, and in time she meets Boaz, who takes her as his bride. The story ends with Naomi cradling her grandson and a new hope-filled future opens for her.

Both Ruth and Naomi have to suffer the literal exile of dwelling in a foreign land, and the emotional exile of bereavement, where those who gave them safety are taken from them. It is Ruth the foreigner who excels in this story. She chooses the way of love even in the vulnerability of exile. And it is in exile that she experiences being the beloved. In exile we can throw up our hands and complain that God has treated us bitterly. Or, like Ruth, we can choose the way of love.

Lord, in my exile help me choose the way of love.

MICHAEL MITTON

Heaven's exiles

Peter, an apostle of Jesus Christ. To the exiles of the Dispersion in Pontus, Galatia, Cappadocia, Asia, and Bithynia, who have been chosen and destined by God the Father and sanctified by the Spirit to be obedient to Jesus Christ and to be sprinkled with his blood: May grace and peace be yours in abundance. Blessed be the God and Father of our Lord Jesus Christ! By his great mercy he has given us a new birth into a living hope through the resurrection of Jesus Christ from the dead.

In this passage, and in 1 Peter 2:11, words are used that are translated in many English versions as 'exile'. Peter clearly held to a view that for those who follow Christ there is something about our existence here on earth that makes us not quite at home in this world. The followers of Jesus carry a destiny that is to do with heaven; they are people who have been spiritually birthed into a new identity due to the resurrection of Jesus. The words Peter employs were often used of someone who lived in a strange land and who carried a homesickness, such that their thoughts often turned to, and their first loyalty was to, that home. It is that yearning for Eden that we met in our earlier reading.

This image of exile describes our relationship with this world to which God has sent us. Jesus often taught about the kingdom of heaven, which is the true place of belonging for his followers. If this is the case, how should we live in this world? If we take the Babylonian exile as an example, then it means we put down roots in this world and learn ways of flourishing as exiles. But we will always hold to the values of the kingdom and this will often throw us into conflict with this world, a conflict that in the end led Jesus to the cross. But the resurrection revealed the true nature of the kingdom of heaven. Exiles can be a wonderful gift to a nation, and the call of heaven's exiles is to bring heaven's resurrection gifts to the land where we dwell.

Lord, make me a blessing to the land where I dwell.

MICHAEL MITTON

Empowered in exile

In those days Jesus came from Nazareth of Galilee and was baptised by John in the Jordan. And just as he was coming up out of the water, he saw the heavens torn apart and the Spirit descending like a dove on him. And a voice came from heaven, 'You are my Son, the Beloved; with you I am well pleased.' And the Spirit immediately drove him out into the wilderness. He was in the wilderness for forty days, tempted by Satan; and he was with the wild beasts; and the angels waited on him.

This passage is how Mark introduces his readers to the person of Jesus. The Son of God's arrival in this world is heralded by the prophet John, who greets him in the waters of the Jordan and plunges him under that flowing river in the ritual of baptism. As Jesus is immersed in the waters of this earth, so heaven opens and out comes none other than the Holy Spirit of God. Surprisingly, the Spirit appears not in an image of mighty power, but in the meek form of a dove – very much like our common wood pigeon. Perhaps one of the reasons that the third person of the Trinity should take such a humble form is that the rock dove is a natural inhabitant of the desert, and it is into that habitat that the Spirit leads Jesus. For Jesus, who is fully human, this environment is a place of exile – it is far from comfortable.

It is a truly fascinating start to the gospel and, among other things, it tells us that the Holy Spirit may well lead any of us into places that feel to us exilic, yet to the Spirit are home. Jesus leads the way for us and shows that, though the place of exile can be tough and there are battles to be had there, it can also be a place of renewal and overcoming. If we allow the Spirit to lead us, we may feel surprisingly at home there.

Holy Spirit, grant me an open heart to follow your pathways.

MICHAEL MITTON

Faith in exile

When [Jesus] entered Capernaum, a centurion came to him, appealing to him and saying, 'Lord, my servant is lying at home paralysed, in terrible distress.' And he said to him, 'I will come and cure him.' The centurion answered, 'Lord, I am not worthy to have you come under my roof; but only speak the word, and my servant will be healed… When Jesus heard him, he was amazed and said to those who followed him, 'Truly I tell you, in no one in Israel have I found such faith.'

Though the people of God returned to the land of Israel after the Babylonian exile, they never felt the land was truly theirs, as it was occupied by a succession of foreign powers. In fact, they still spoke of this experience as exile – they could not be truly at home in their homeland. At the time of Jesus, those responsible for this 'exile' were the Romans and they were regarded as oppressors who tainted the precious holy land with their Gentile presence.

Today's story involves one such Roman – a senior soldier who, much to everyone's surprise, comes to Jesus for help. Those watching would have eagerly expected Jesus to take full opportunity in this encounter for proclaiming fearful judgements on this defiant pagan who was polluting the land. Instead, Jesus does quite the opposite. He not only heals the servant of the centurion, but he then commends this Gentile oppressor for having more faith about him than the most pious of the religious establishment. This would not have gone down well with that establishment!

But Jesus noticed the activity of the Spirit in that centurion's heart. The Spirit was at work in the desert. The Romans may have been the perpetrators of exile, but even that did not put them out of reach of God's grace. For Jesus, exile was not about land and power. Anyone who lacked faith was in exile. The one growing in faith was on the journey home.

At any point in life we can feel oppressed by others. But there may be times when the oppressor experiences a raw human need, as did that centurion. Such moments can create openings for extraordinary faith.

Lord, keep my eyes always open to signs of faith in unexpected places.

MICHAEL MITTON

Revelation in exile

Now when Jesus came into the district of Caesarea Philippi, he asked his disciples, 'Who do people say that the Son of Man is?'... Simon Peter answered, 'You are the Messiah, the Son of the living God.' And Jesus answered him, 'Blessed are you, Simon son of Jonah! For flesh and blood has not revealed this to you, but my Father in heaven. And I tell you, you are Peter, and on this rock I will build my church, and the gates of Hades will not prevail against it.'

In today's story, Jesus has taken his disciples on a long journey north to the city of Caesarea Philippi. This was an area full of ancient temples dedicated to the worship of Baal, and it was also the centre of Pan worship. Herod also built there a huge temple for the worship of Caesar. It is a rocky place and visitors today can still see the opening to the great chasm that was believed to be the gateway to Hades. The disciples were no doubt disturbed that Jesus should lead them to such an unholy place.

And yet here in this very place, which would have felt very much like an exile place to the disciples, Jesus, in the affirmation of Peter, reveals himself to be the Messiah, the Son of God. And not only this, but here he plants his church, using the analogy of the great rocks of the place, even referring to the gates of Hades.

This story is full of symbolism and meaning, but perhaps one of the messages that Jesus was conveying to his disciples was his desire that his church was to be present and active in the very places that upright, religious people chose to avoid. In such places Jesus wished to reveal his glory through the witness of the church. Here he would see to it that the gates that imprisoned so many people would give way to the power of the gospel.

It is all too easy to write some places off as ungodly, and yet these may be the very places where Jesus wishes to make his presence felt. And he does this through you and me – his church.

Lord Jesus, let your glory shine through me today.

MICHAEL MITTON

Praise in exile

After they had given them a severe flogging, they threw them into prison and ordered the jailer to keep them securely. Following these instructions, he put them in the innermost cell and fastened their feet in the stocks. About midnight Paul and Silas were praying and singing hymns to God, and the prisoners were listening to them. Suddenly there was an earthquake, so violent that the foundations of the prison were shaken; and immediately all the doors were opened and everyone's chains were unfastened.

Paul and Silas are on one of their great mission trips, and in this story we find them in Philippi, a mostly Gentile city in eastern Macedonia. Their stay in this city is focused around three people: Lydia, from the higher echelons of that society; a slave girl, who was regarded as barely human; and the jailer, a Roman citizen from the middle classes. Paul and Silas have clearly become at home with all strata of society.

However, there is no shortage of people who are opposed to these evangelists, and it is not long before Paul and Silas find themselves flogged and thrown into jail. The severe flogging was enough to kill some people. They survive, but have to spend the night in chains in the foul inner cell. A more hostile exile is hard to imagine. And yet, despite the pain, darkness and imprisonment, we find Paul and Silas singing at the tops of their voices as if they are at a Christian summer celebration. You wonder how they manage to 'sing the Lord's song in a foreign land' (Psalm 137:4). Clearly some work of grace has seeped so deeply into their hearts that an inner world has become more powerful than the outer world they inhabit. From the inner cells of their hearts they praise and worship God.

Some exiles can feel very hostile. But any one of us can reach into the inner cells of our own hearts and find there the presence of the one who truly sets us free. The Holy Spirit delights to lead us to such places, for where the Spirit is, there is freedom (2 Corinthians 3:17).

---

*Lord, when I feel imprisoned, let me follow the trail of your Spirit
to find true freedom.*

MICHAEL MITTON

The body in exile

For while we are still in this tent, we groan under our burden, because we wish not to be unclothed but to be further clothed, so that what is mortal may be swallowed up by life. He who has prepared us for this very thing is God, who has given us the Spirit as a guarantee. So we are always confident; even though we know that while we are at home in the body we are away from the Lord – for we walk by faith, not by sight.

Today's passage is part of a complex piece of Paul's correspondence with the Christians in Corinth. One of the questions that arose in that infant church was quite what to do with the body, with all its lusts and appetites. It seems there were some who thought that following Christ gave licence to give in to these appetites (1 Corinthians 6:12–20). There were almost certainly others who would have been influenced by those Greek and Roman philosophers who saw the soul as a higher creature weighed down by the rebellious body. It was not just the first-century Christians who struggled with this – the human body has troubled the church in every generation since. Quite what do we do with it when it lets us down?

In 1 Corinthians 15 Paul introduces the notion of the resurrection body. If you take this into account, today's passage seems to suggest that we need to regard our present bodies as temporary in the grand scheme of things. If we settle down too much in this body, we run the risk of being so focused on it that we drift away from the Lord. On the other hand, these bodies will one day in Christ be transformed into something truly glorious, and for that reason they should be honoured and appreciated. In one respect dwelling in this mortal body is a sign of our exile. As we have seen, it is possible to flourish in exile, but we never cease our yearning for our true home. The vision of our future home can transform our present exile.

Lord, let me be a good steward of the body you have entrusted to me for my sojourn in this world.

MICHAEL MITTON

God in exile

Do nothing from selfish ambition or conceit, but in humility regard others as better than yourselves… Let the same mind be in you that was in Christ Jesus, who, though he was in the form of God, did not regard equality with God as something to be exploited, but emptied himself, taking the form of a slave, being born in human likeness. And being found in human form, he humbled himself and became obedient to the point of death – even death on a cross.

In some churches, at a Communion service the congregation says the words of the Nicene Creed, which includes these words about Jesus: 'For us and for our salvation he came down from heaven, was incarnate from the Holy Spirit and was made man.' It goes on to say that 'he ascended into heaven'. The early writers of our creed would have been influenced by such passages as today's reading from Philippians. This is a well-known passage that describes the humbling of Jesus, who descended from the glorious habitation of heaven to this broken world, and who lived and died among us before returning to his natural homeland. In other words, while he was with us in his incarnated form, he was living in exile.

As we think about his life as an exile, we see that Jesus most certainly flourished in this world. Though he 'emptied himself', he lived life to the full. He did not behave as a visitor – he made himself at home. He was born into the world and spent time growing up from an infant into a teenager and adult. He put down roots and made friends. He learned the language of the people. But he also kept talking about his homeland, and demonstrating what it was like. He spoke about it in such a way that something lit up in the hearts of the people, so much so that they started to long to visit his homeland. In time he explained that he had opened the door for all who wished to follow him to be part of that home.

Jesus' time in exile cost him his life. But imagine where we would be now had he chosen to stay at home!

Dear Jesus, thank you for making yourself at home in my world.

MICHAEL MITTON

108

God at home

Then I saw a new heaven and a new earth; for the first heaven and the first earth had passed away, and the sea was no more. And I saw the holy city, the new Jerusalem, coming down out of heaven from God, prepared as a bride adorned for her husband. And I heard a loud voice from the throne saying, 'See, the home of God is among mortals. He will dwell with them; they will be his peoples, and God himself will be with them.'

The writer of the book of Revelation is called John, and he tells us that he is writing from the island of Patmos (Revelation 1:9), which was probably a Roman penal settlement. He is therefore an author writing in exile and, as we saw with Ezekiel, living in exile provides a fertile environment for prophetic visions. In the earlier chapters of his book he details specific prophecies for local churches, but as the book moves on he covers a much wider sweep of cosmic history. In his spirit he sees terrifying judgements on the earth that culminate in a triumphant defeat of Satan, death and Hades (Revelation 20). This leads on to a most beautiful vision of the new heaven and new earth, and we are treated to a glorious vision of a healed and reformed universe with God once again dwelling fully with his created humans. We have returned to paradise and the exile from that garden is finally over.

What is particularly wonderful and extraordinary is the cry that John hears coming from the throne of God, which declares that 'the home of God is among mortals'. However we understand this mysterious prophecy of the last times, this cry from heaven is utterly heart-warming. It tells us that the place where God feels most at home is among mortals. There is perhaps no vision more compelling than this one to declare that God is most at home when he is in the company of the humans he created. He therefore yearns for that day when he can fully dwell with us again. Until that time we are all in a season of exile, but an exile full of possibility and promise.

Even so, come, Lord Jesus.

MICHAEL MITTON

To Calvary and beyond

Starting on the Fifth Sunday of Lent, the readings for the next two weeks trace Jesus' journey to Jerusalem with his disciples and what happened there. We follow Luke's account, with references to the other gospels, while I occasionally take episodes out of their narrative sequence in order to draw out a theme or emphasis.

Luke is a superb storyteller, with vividly portrayed people and settings, and it is no surprise that – out of the four gospels – his version of events is often the most familiar. He uses contrast to make a point, pairing stories of repentance with stubbornness, humility with pride, belief with unbelief. He also highlights the favourable responses of those who, for a variety of reasons, are marginal to the society of the time – whose physical or material condition, gender or religious status place them 'at the edges'.

Time and again, it is these 'edge' people, the marginal figures, who take a step forward in understanding at least something of who Jesus is and what he is talking about. Over the next fortnight, we will meet a blind beggar, a tax collector and a Roman centurion (among others), who each respond wholeheartedly to the invitation held out to them by the Son of God. Despite (or maybe because of) who they are, they 'get it' in a way that a certain rich man, and representatives of the religious authorities, and – most depressingly – Jesus' own disciples do not 'get it'.

We can assume too easily that we would not have made the same mistake. Reading these familiar stories, we can be tempted to congratulate ourselves that we would have understood right from the start, because here we are reading *New Daylight* as present-day followers of Jesus. But a moment's reflection on life – and especially on our life as the body of Christ in our local churches – shows that we can miss the point and get things wrong as easily as Peter and the other eleven disciples. There is always more for us to learn of God and the ways of God's working in the world.

As I have prepared these readings, Henry Wansbrough's commentary on Luke (BRF, 1998) has been a particular help.

NAOMI STARKEY

The disciples don't understand

Jesus took the Twelve aside and told them, 'We are going up to Jerusalem, and everything that is written by the prophets about the Son of Man will be fulfilled. He will be handed over to the Gentiles. They will mock him, insult him and spit on him; they will flog him and kill him. On the third day he will rise again.' The disciples did not understand any of this. Its meaning was hidden from them, and they did not know what he was talking about.

Today, the Fifth Sunday of Lent, was traditionally designated 'Passion Sunday', although this designation has now generally lapsed. Worshippers had the opportunity to start reflecting on the 'passion' or suffering of Jesus before Palm Sunday began the countdown through Holy Week to Good Friday itself.

Our Bible reading is a salutary reminder that there is more to suffering than physical pain – because Jesus would surely have been grieved by his disciples' failure to understand what would happen to him. At this late stage in his ministry, he tells them in unflinching detail exactly what he will endure on their forthcoming visit to the capital city: mocked, insulted, flogged and killed at the hands of the Gentiles. But his own followers, his closest friends, 'did not know what he was talking about'.

If we are ever tempted to despair because of our fellow Christians, if we are ever overwhelmed by frustration at other people's inability to understand the good news, we can imagine, just a little, the loneliness that must have lain at the heart of Jesus' ministry. As we will read in a few days, 'the Son of Man came to seek and to save the lost' (Luke 19:10), yet even those who were part of his band of disciples continued to flounder and be lost in confusion as to what Jesus' work was actually about.

Loving Lord Jesus, friend and brother, help us when we struggle to make sense of your call and your purposes for our lives. Give us patience with those among whom we live and worship and minister, that when they fail to grasp your truth, we can walk together with them into your light.

NAOMI STARKEY

The children understand

People were also bringing babies to Jesus for him to place his hands on them. When the disciples saw this, they rebuked them. But Jesus called the children to him and said, 'Let the little children come to me, and do not hinder them, for the kingdom of God belongs to such as these. Truly I tell you, anyone who will not receive the kingdom of God like a little child will never enter it.'

This is a popular Bible reading for services of infant (and child) baptism – and it may well bring to mind a happy, sunlit scene of Jesus surrounded by smiling youngsters. Such a scene is entirely possible, of course, but we should not let it beguile us away from the sharp point that the gospel writer is making here.

Luke's gospel is flavoured with a bias towards the poor, marginalised and overlooked parts of the community – a bias evident in the subversive text known as the Magnificat. Mary's song of praise (Luke 1:46–55), proclaimed while visiting her cousin Elizabeth, speaks of scattering the proud and sending 'the rich away empty'. That same note of defiance is clear in this apparently homely episode of Jesus and the children – because, says Jesus as he overrules his high-handed disciples, 'the kingdom of God belongs to such as these'.

Stop and read those words again: the kingdom of God, no less, 'belongs' to 'such as these'. Jesus does not say that there is room for the children too, that they can be squeezed in somewhere, provided they're quiet and well-behaved. He says that the kingdom belongs to them, to the children. And we should remember that children were not indulged and treasured as they are in many parts of the world today. They were weak, economically unproductive and tolerated at best or (as here) ordered out of the way. Jesus' words are breathtaking in their rebuke to his culture's norms and practices.

Loving Lord Jesus, friend and brother, we pray for the grace and humility to grasp what it means to receive your kingdom as little children. Challenge our pride and shake up our complacency so that we are changed to become truly fit for your purposes.

NAOMI STARKEY

The blind man understands

As Jesus approached Jericho, a blind man was sitting by the roadside begging... He called out, 'Jesus, Son of David, have mercy on me!'... Jesus asked him, 'What do you want me to do for you?' 'Lord, I want to see,' he replied. Jesus said to him, 'Receive your sight; your faith has healed you.' Immediately he received his sight and followed Jesus, praising God. When all the people saw it, they also praised God.

Here is another example of Luke's bias towards the poor and underprivileged: the story of a blind beggar, named as Bartimaeus in Mark's version of this episode (Mark 10:46–52). Unlike so many others, this blind man sees clearly that Jesus is no ordinary rabbi, naming him 'Son of David', an important messianic title in the other gospels.

It's striking that Jesus does not automatically rush in as saviour in the situation, even though the physical need is so evident. Instead, as he stands before this sightless man, who has been reduced to seeking favours from passers-by, Jesus asks, 'What do you want me to do for you?' The man has been shouting for 'mercy', so he needs to clarify what form he wants this mercy to take, says the Son of David.

This straight question is given a straight answer, and Jesus' response is equally direct. The beggar receives his sight 'immediately' and a moment later Jesus is on his way to Jericho again, this time with a new follower whose overflowing gratitude affects the crowd. Despite Jesus' grim predictions of death just a few verses earlier (see Sunday's comment), his ministry's popularity and success must have seemed gratifyingly unstoppable to his disciples at this point.

The formerly blind man also sees that Jesus' healing action calls for a deeper response than a mere thank you. We don't know whether he simply followed Jesus down the Jericho road for a while or whether he ended up joining the wider band of disciples. Either way, the encounter changed the direction of his life.

Imagine Jesus standing before you, asking 'What do you want me to do for you?' What would your reply be?

NAOMI STARKEY

The wealthy tax collector understands...

But Zacchaeus stood up and said to the Lord, 'Look, Lord! Here and now
I give half of my possessions to the poor, and if I have cheated anybody
out of anything, I will pay back four times the amount.' Jesus said to
him, 'Today salvation has come to this house, because this man, too, is
a son of Abraham. For the Son of Man came to seek and to save the lost.'

Jesus is now passing through Jericho, where he meets Zacchaeus in the
much-loved story of the wealthy tax collector who climbs a sycamore tree
so that he can see over the crowd. The old Sunday school song (with
actions) that tells of this 'very little man' makes it all sound rather sweet
as Jesus invites himself round 'for tea', as if he was making a play date
with a friendless child.

In fact, Zacchaeus would have been a deeply unpopular local figure
because he was in effect a collaborator with the Roman occupiers. It
wasn't a matter of working for the equivalent of a governmental tax
department; he was siding with the enemy of his own people – and lining
his pockets at the same time. The onlooking crowd, who a few verses
back had been praising God at the healing of the blind man, now begin to
mutter against Jesus for mixing with this social outcast (v. 7).

Jesus, however, offers Zacchaeus robust affirmation. Not only does he
demand and receive an invitation to his home, but he affirms him as a
'son of Abraham' – an explicit reminder to the crowd that the ways of the
kingdom are ways of radical hospitality, radical belonging, extending to
those whom we would very much prefer to avoid. Notice, though, that
this affirmation comes after the tax collector's public self-humbling.
Zacchaeus basically admits that he has been a cheat but promises to pay
back fourfold, which went beyond what the law demanded. Further to
this, and without even being asked by Jesus, he promises to halve his
personal wealth to benefit the poor.

Like the crowd, we slip into expecting God to work on our terms,
following our agenda. Let's pray to remain always open to the
full extent of God's mind-boggling grace and generosity.

NAOMI STARKEY

... but the wealthy ruler doesn't

[Jesus] said to [the ruler], 'You still lack one thing. Sell everything you have and give to the poor, and you will have treasure in heaven. Then come, follow me.' When he heard this, he became very sad, because he was very wealthy. Jesus looked at him and said, 'How hard it is for the rich to enter the kingdom of God! Indeed, it is easier for a camel to go through the eye of a needle than for someone who is rich to enter the kingdom of God.' Those who heard this asked, 'Who then can be saved?' Jesus replied, 'What is impossible with man is possible with God.'

As mentioned in the introduction, another characteristic of Luke's gospel is using contrast as a teaching method. In line with that approach, we're returning to the previous chapter to find a very different story to that of Zacchaeus. While the tax collector announces a halving of his wealth as well as an astonishingly generous payback for his old cheating ways, the ruler here responds very differently to his encounter with Jesus. It's true that he faces a daunting challenge: selling up and distributing all his property to the poor. His response to this challenge is emotional, a deep sadness at the cost of following Jesus, one which (it would seem) he is not prepared to pay.

The message that Jesus draws out was as countercultural then as it is today. The Hebrew scriptures taught that prosperity was a sign of God's blessing. How did that relate to wealthy people's being as good as barred from God's kingdom? The vivid image of a camel struggling to get through the eye of a needle (whether a metaphorical needle or a real, and narrow, gateway) was to underline the impossibility of the challenge, not to suggest that there might be a way round it.

We may hear this story and worry that God is making some impossible-sounding demand of us, something that feels just too costly. We should remember that God is our loving Father in heaven who gives good gifts to those who ask him (Matthew 7:11).

Father, help me to trust – and not fear – your calling on my life.

NAOMI STARKEY

The religious authorities refuse to understand

One day as Jesus was teaching the people in the temple courts and proclaiming the good news, the chief priests and the teachers of the law, together with the elders, came up to him. 'Tell us by what authority you are doing these things,' they said… He replied, 'I will also ask you a question. Tell me: John's baptism – was it from heaven, or of human origin?'… They answered, 'We don't know where it was from.' Jesus said, 'Neither will I tell you by what authority I am doing these things.'

Clearly every local religious authority 'big gun' lines up here to check out the credentials of this suspiciously popular local rabbi. What's his background? Where did he train? Is he 'sound'? This wasn't just a matter of making sure that he wasn't peddling heresy. They were challenging Jesus' authority as a teacher and, fundamentally, trying to trick him into incriminating himself in some way.

Jesus is wary of their barely concealed malice and, instead of answering their question politely, he comes back with a counter-question that confounds them. He then brings the exchange to an end and goes off to carry on his ministry. What follows (vv. 9–19) is the pointed parable of the vineyard tenants who reject the owner's authority and go so far as to kill his son. After that, these same religious leaders start to plot Jesus' arrest.

Why can the very people supposedly most tuned in to the ways of God not receive his Messiah? Why don't they respond to his teaching with the crowd's edge-of-the-seat excitement? As for so many, now as then, with a vested interest in the status quo, the prospect of change is threatening for them. They would rather seek ways of ignoring or marginalising the new teaching than test their assumptions against it. As far as recognising God's Messiah, assumptions are very firmly in place – and this young man from Nazareth most certainly does not fit. That God might be in the business of surprises does not seem to have occurred to them.

Lord Jesus, open our hearts by your Spirit so that we are ready to be surprised by you.

NAOMI STARKEY

Beware future misunderstanding

Some of his disciples were remarking about how the temple was adorned with beautiful stones and with gifts dedicated to God. But Jesus said, 'As for what you see here, the time will come when not one stone will be left on another; every one of them will be thrown down.' 'Teacher,' they asked, 'when will these things happen? And what will be the sign that they are about to take place?' He replied: 'Watch out that you are not deceived. For many will come in my name, claiming, "I am he," and, "The time is near." Do not follow them.'

Imagine being on a pilgrimage to St Paul's in London or St Peter's in Rome and commenting to your group leader on the stunning architecture – and getting the response, 'Make the most of it! It's going to be demolished in a few years' time.' The disciples would have been even more shocked hearing Jesus' response to their pleasantries about the temple. The temple was not just the national place of worship but was also seen as the dwelling place of God himself. It's where Jesus himself lingered as a boy, because it was his 'Father's house' (Luke 2:49).

Following the Jewish revolt in AD66, the temple was destroyed, never to be rebuilt. And, as Jesus had warned, in the decades before that cataclysm there was a rise in messianic movements, offering false hope and misleading instruction. Given the disciples' less-than-unblemished track record of understanding Jesus' teaching, the likelihood of their being led astray would have seemed fairly high.

We find warnings about false teaching throughout the scriptures, from Old Testament fulminations against Baal worship to the warnings in Paul's letters against the 'Judaisers' in the early years of the church. People seem to have a habit of going off on their own forays of belief. While asking questions about our faith is an essential part of growing to maturity in Christ, it is often hard to agree on what should constitute the non-negotiables of belief.

How can we maintain a good balance between cultivating a flexible and informed faith and avoiding false teaching? And how widely should we range in defining what we mean by 'false'?

NAOMI STARKEY

Jerusalem doesn't understand

As [Jesus] approached Jerusalem and saw the city, he wept over it and said, 'If you, even you, had only known on this day what would bring you peace – but now it is hidden from your eyes. The days will come upon you when your enemies will build an embankment against you and encircle you and hem you in on every side. They will dash you to the ground, you and the children within your walls. They will not leave one stone on another, because you did not recognise the time of God's coming to you.'

To mark Palm Sunday, the beginning of Holy Week, we step back in the flow of the gospel story to an emotional scene that takes place shortly after the triumphal entry. Immediately preceding our passage, verses 28 to 40 tell the familiar story of Jesus' arrival in Jerusalem, riding from the Mount of Olives on a borrowed colt. That is a story full of drama and triumph and loud hosannas, cloaks spread on the road to make a royal welcome and also (unsurprisingly) disapproving Pharisees muttering on the sidelines. It's the climax to which this gospel has been building since chapter 9, when Jesus 'resolutely set out for Jerusalem' (Luke 9:51).

Now, straight after triumph, there is weeping. Jesus looks out over Jerusalem and speaks words of lament that echo the lamentations spoken long ago by the Old Testament prophets. Just as they bewailed Israel and Judah's indifference to their warnings, so Jesus mourns the city's failure to heed the good news that he has brought. The place of the temple, the 'Father's house', does not recognise the Lord's anointed one.

As we've already seen, the religious leaders reject Jesus' teaching. As we will reflect later this week, in doing so they influence the people to reject him too, and hosannas will become shouts of 'Crucify!' Imagine what might have happened if the 'chief priests and the teachers of the law' who met to condemn Jesus (Luke 22:66–71) had instead hailed him as Messiah.

Pray for those who lead your local church, for local councillors and for other community leaders, that God will bless them with patience, compassion and wisdom in their plans and decisions.

NAOMI STARKEY

Understanding and misunderstanding at the temple

When Jesus entered the temple courts, he began to drive out those who were selling. 'It is written,' he said to them, '"My house will be a house of prayer"; but you have made it "a den of robbers"'… [Jesus] saw the rich putting their gifts into the temple treasury. He also saw a poor widow put in two very small copper coins. 'Truly I tell you,' he said, 'this poor widow has put in more than all the others. All these people gave their gifts out of their wealth; but she out of her poverty put in all she had to live on.'

Here are two strongly contrasting scenes at the temple. First, Jesus drives out the 'sellers' to remind them of the temple's rightful purpose. Second, he draws attention to one of the poorest of the poor who makes the boldest of financial gestures. Both scenes inspire and also challenge us.

Jesus' treatment of the temple sellers sounds calculated to offend. Luke does not indicate that they were doing anything other than conducting normal business – but seeking the presence of the living God requires setting aside 'normal business'. What should our response be in terms of our local 'houses of prayer'? Close the church bookstall? Stop charging for cathedral entry? There are no easy answers.

The irony of the widow's story is that she put all her money into the very repository intended to support those in her position. Throughout the scriptures, widows are singled out as in need of special care, but this woman's generosity gives her the dignity of being able to give to others. Remember the wealthy ruler in Luke 18? Here is one of the most vulnerable members of the same society doing exactly what he could not countenance doing.

'Father, hallowed be your name, your kingdom come. Give us each day our daily bread' (Luke 11:2–3). Think about how to make more space for prayer in your local church. Think, too, about how you can learn to depend more on God for your daily needs, thus freeing yourself to bless and be blessed in giving to others.

NAOMI STARKEY

The crowds don't really understand

Every day [Jesus] was teaching at the temple. But the chief priests, the teachers of the law and the leaders among the people were trying to kill him. Yet they could not find any way to do it, because all the people hung on his words... But the whole crowd shouted, 'Away with this man! Release Barabbas to us!' (Barabbas had been thrown into prison for an insurrection in the city, and for murder.) Wanting to release Jesus, Pilate appealed to them again. But they kept shouting, 'Crucify him! Crucify him!'... So Pilate decided to grant their demand.

Here we have two violently contrasting scenes. The first follows immediately from Jesus' ejecting of the sellers from the temple. Commercial bustle has been replaced by a rapt audience, hanging on the words of the rabbi from Nazareth. The city is busy with pilgrims gathering for the Passover, many of whom would remember Jesus' dramatic entry surrounded by a cheering throng. This is the point, surely, when Jesus' authority is acclaimed on a wider stage than ever before. Even the scheming leaders seem to have been thwarted! What can possibly go wrong?

Cut to a scene just days later, at the headquarters of Pilate, the Roman governor of Judea. The crowd are baying for Jesus' blood, demanding a particularly barbaric form of execution. Maybe his supporters have been drowned out by the mob. Or perhaps the whole gathering has been orchestrated by those scheming leaders! What on earth has gone wrong?

Even though Jesus rejected the temptation of instant fame at the start of his ministry (Luke 4:5–12), now he is subjected to the brutal swing of popular mood. Over recent years social media has shown how fast adulation can turn to vilification. A film clip or photograph goes viral, spreads around the globe in a few hours, and dizzying fame – or infamy – results for the subjects. People who seek such fame or infamy should beware the personal cost; leaders who invoke 'the will of the people' should beware how fickle that 'will' can be.

Lord, keep us mindful of the risks of following the crowd,
whatever that crowd might be.

NAOMI STARKEY

Judas' tragic failure to understand

Now the Festival of Unleavened Bread, called the Passover, was approaching, and the chief priests and the teachers of the law were looking for some way to get rid of Jesus, for they were afraid of the people. Then Satan entered Judas, called Iscariot, one of the Twelve. And Judas went to the chief priests and the officers of the temple guard and discussed with them how he might betray Jesus. They were delighted and agreed to give him money. He consented, and watched for an opportunity to hand Jesus over to them when no crowd was present.

It's easy to reduce Judas to the pantomime baddie of the Easter story, playing a comparably bloodstained role to Herod at Christmas. On the other hand, mention of Satan entering Judas has led to fruitless speculation about his being 'possessed by the devil', as if Judas became a kind of horror-movie zombie, hell-bent on evil.

We don't know exactly why Judas betrayed Jesus, although that hasn't stopped the airing of many theories. Some would portray him as a disappointed freedom fighter, sacrificing his leader for failing to live up to expectations. Others consider him simply a wicked man. John's gospel takes a generally dim view of Judas, summarising him as 'a thief; as keeper of the money bag, he used to help himself to what was put into it' (John 12:6). Yet others would pity him, seeing him as the helpless puppet of God's purposes, damned so that the world might be saved.

'What could possibly go wrong?' I asked yesterday, reflecting on the crowd's eager support of Jesus. Here is the answer: one of his own followers collaborates with his enemies to isolate him from his fans and deliver him into the hands of those enemies. Judas didn't understand that he had free will, that he didn't have to listen to the voice of the accuser, the father of lies. He didn't understand – and he chose to walk in darkness instead of in the light.

Sometimes betrayal is cold-blooded deception to get the best of an opponent. Perhaps, more often, we allow betrayal to grow through half-truths, self-justifications and failing to admit our selfish motives.

NAOMI STARKEY

The disciples still don't understand

[Jesus] withdrew about a stone's throw beyond [the disciples], knelt down and prayed, 'Father, if you are willing, take this cup from me; yet not my will, but yours be done.' An angel from heaven appeared to him and strengthened him. And being in anguish, he prayed more earnestly, and his sweat was like drops of blood falling to the ground. When he rose from prayer and went back to the disciples, he found them asleep, exhausted from sorrow. 'Why are you sleeping?' he asked them. 'Get up and pray so that you will not fall into temptation.'

Jesus has eaten a last Passover with his friends; he has shared wine with them and broken bread; he has calmed a dispute as to who is the greatest; he has warned Simon Peter of that forthright disciple's inner frailty. Even so, Simon Peter does not acknowledge the truth of his Lord's words until forced by bitter circumstances to do so. He does not understand himself.

Church services on this Maundy Thursday often involve a quiet Eucharist, perhaps some foot-washing, and an hour or two of candle-lit vigil. Such traditions could end up downplaying the knife-edge uncertainty described in our passage. Jesus is 'in anguish', sweating profusely, praying earnestly – we could say desperately. Waking his sleeping disciples, he orders them to pray too, so as to escape temptation. What does he fear for them – that they will leave him? Deny him? Join Judas in siding with his enemies?

The impression is that they still don't grasp the full immensity of the events unfolding. They are 'exhausted from sorrow', perhaps troubled by Jesus' anguish, and are asleep, maybe trusting that things will be better in the morning. After all, they have two swords in case of trouble (v. 38)! They don't understand – but at least they are faithful, according to Luke. In Mark's account (14:50), every single one of them runs away.

Lord God, we may not have discovered our full strength; we may be unaware of how weak we really are. Either way, help us to know ourselves better and show us how we may best serve you, just as we are.

NAOMI STARKEY

The centurion understands

It was now about noon, and darkness came over the whole land until three in the afternoon, for the sun stopped shining. And the curtain of the temple was torn in two. Jesus called out with a loud voice, 'Father, into your hands I commit my spirit.' When he had said this, he breathed his last. The centurion, seeing what had happened, praised God and said, 'Surely this was a righteous man.' When all the people who had gathered to witness this sight saw what took place, they beat their breasts and went away.

Good Friday… and as the Son of God hangs dying, so darkness comes at noon. Luke indicates that this was a natural event – an eclipse – but it was also one of the signs of the 'day of the Lord', as described by the prophet Amos. According to Amos, the Sovereign Lord declares: 'I will make the sun go down at noon and darken the earth in broad daylight… I will make that time like mourning for an only son and the end of it like a bitter day' (Amos 8:9–10).

It is a 'bitter day' indeed, and yet God's plan for redemption is completed in Jesus' death. Matthew mentions an earthquake (Matthew 27:51–53), perhaps the trigger for the tearing of the temple curtain also mentioned by Luke. This tearing could be another example of a natural phenomenon that is powerfully symbolic, as the barriers between humanity and God are swept aside.

A centurion stands on duty, observing the brutal and strange events of that Friday afternoon – and somehow he understands. Luke's version of his declaration is less forthright than Mark's – where he says, 'Surely this man was the Son of God!' (Mark 15:39) – but still shows clearly that this Gentile, this member of the occupying military force, sees that here was no ordinary criminal or rebel suffering a cruel death. This was 'a righteous man'.

The crowd see what has happened and express their grief and regret – too late to make a difference. Let us pray to be so attuned to God's purposes in the world that we understand more often than we misunderstand.

NAOMI STARKEY

Joseph of Arimathea understands

Now there was a man named Joseph, a member of the Council, a good and upright man, who had not consented to their decision and action. He came from the Judean town of Arimathea, and he himself was wait-ing for the kingdom of God. Going to Pilate, he asked for Jesus' body. Then he took it down, wrapped it in linen cloth and placed it in a tomb cut in the rock, one in which no one had yet been laid. It was Preparation Day, and the Sabbath was about to begin.

Here's a shock: Joseph is a council member, a key figure in the religious establishment, whose distance from their scheming against Jesus is spelled out clearly. He also appears in John's gospel as 'a disciple of Jesus, but secretly because he feared the Jewish leaders', and in that account of Jesus' death, he does the work of burial with Nicodemus, who had 'visited Jesus at night' (John 19:38–39).

Thanks to the social and religious standing of these men, Jesus is buried with a level of reverence and respect that would not normally have been accorded to a criminal after public execution. Note the detail that the tomb had not been used for any other interments. This is not just a matter of its being a fitting place for the Lord to lie, but to underline the fact that there could be no mix-up as to which body had gone missing on Easter morning. There had only ever been one body in that tomb – the body of Jesus.

Disciples (whether secret or not) are needed in positions of power and influence in society. They can use their power and influence to do good deeds, which may run counter to the values of that society, while not cast-ing those disciples in the role of revolutionaries. Those whose calling it is to campaign on the front line against injustice, at whatever cost to them-selves, should refrain from judging those who work behind the scenes.

---

*Father in heaven, keep us from trying to be what we are not,
out of dissatisfaction with who we are. May we understand and accept
whom you have created and called us to be.*

NAOMI STARKEY

Understanding dawns for all

On the first day of the week, very early in the morning, the women took the spices they had prepared and went to the tomb. They found the stone rolled away from the tomb, but when they entered, they did not find the body of the Lord Jesus. While they were wondering about this, suddenly two men in clothes that gleamed like lightning stood beside them. In their fright the women bowed down with their faces to the ground, but the men said to them, 'Why do you look for the living among the dead? He is not here; he has risen!'

At last, it is the day of resurrection, the third day after Jesus was delivered 'to the hands of sinners [and] crucified' (v. 7). But the women coming to the tomb – including Mary Magdalene, Joanna and Mary the mother of James – do not remember Jesus' promise of being 'raised again' until the men in shining clothes remind them (v. 8).

Remembering does not necessarily equate to believing, however. Luke tells how they go to the remaining eleven of the inner circle of disciples and report what has happened (presumably also repeating Jesus' promise). The reaction is that they are judged to be speaking 'nonsense' (v. 11), although Peter does make a trip to the tomb, finds it empty and puzzles over the possible implications. Could Jesus have been speaking the truth about himself all along?

In the end, the light of understanding dawns for him and for the rest of the disciples. On the day of Pentecost, the fire of the Spirit (Acts 2:3) ignites their hearts with courage and gives them the words to begin sharing with the whole world God's plan of salvation. As the apostle Paul wrote a few years later: 'We declare God's wisdom, a mystery that has been hidden and that God destined for our glory before time began' (1 Corinthians 2:7).

Our faith rests in a mystery – but a revealed mystery. We believe and trust in God incarnate, not a remote nameless deity. Understanding these truths is the task of a lifetime; salvation, meanwhile, is God's gift to us.

Lord, I believe; help me overcome my unbelief (see Mark 9:24).

NAOMI STARKEY

The risen Jesus

It is a truth universally acknowledged, as Jane Austen would say, that Jesus' tomb was found to be empty on the Sunday morning following his crucifixion. The fact is asserted by all four gospels and cannot seriously be disputed on historical grounds. But where was he? Had he literally been raised bodily from death? Or was his body stolen by grave robbers? Was he not actually dead in the first place? Did he perhaps revive and escape from the tomb? Was it all a well-planned deception carried out by his followers? In whatever way one answers those questions, the fact remains that the empty tomb itself is not conclusive proof of the resurrection.

But all speculation can be laid to rest: Jesus' conquest of death would be manifested among the living. The New Testament attests to perhaps eleven separate encounters with the risen Jesus, some involving single individuals, one a group of more than 500. Their diverse nature makes it impossible to dismiss them as hallucinations, and the difficulty of piecing together all the conflicting accounts only makes it less likely that there was any deliberate collusion in perpetrating a hoax.

Jesus rose with a body that was solidly physical and could be touched. He was able to break bread and eat, and he could be mistaken for a gardener or fellow traveller. At the same time, however, his body was set free from the normal limitations of time and space: he could pass through closed doors; he could appear and disappear at will.

For some weeks Jesus continued to appear to his followers in this way and convinced them of his victory over death. But more than that, his words and actions were to shape them for what lay ahead. After the discovery of the empty tomb, they were speechless and afraid (Mark 16:8), dismissive and unbelieving (Luke 24:11), a dispirited band of supporters fearful of what the future might hold for them. But that was all to change. So, for the next nine days, let's follow the events that transformed this frightened and demoralised group of disciples into a confident and prayerful company of apostles waiting with quiet assurance for the coming of the Holy Spirit and the power to continue God's mission that Jesus had begun.

TIM HEATON

The reconciler

But the angel said to the women, 'Do not be afraid; I know that you are looking for Jesus who was crucified. He is not here; for he has been raised, as he said. Come, see the place where he lay…' So they left the tomb quickly with fear and great joy, and ran to tell his disciples. Suddenly Jesus met them and said, 'Greetings!' And they came to him, took hold of his feet, and worshipped him. Then Jesus said to them, 'Do not be afraid; go and tell my brothers to go to Galilee; there they will see me.'

There is a legend in Christianity that the sun danced before God on the first Easter morning. The resurrection was not for humankind alone and the joy was shared by the whole of creation. Long ago in Christendom, families would get up before dawn on Easter Day and wait to see the sun do a jig as it rose above the rim of the earth. Children were warned not to look directly at the sun but at its reflection in water, perhaps a trough or a pond, and a stone dropped in to ripple the surface always managed to make the sun dance!

They were both called Mary, these women who came to continue their vigil at the tomb at dawn on Sunday. One was Mary Magdalene, the other an unknown Mary, the mother of James and Joseph. We don't know if they saw the dance of the sun, but we do know they were the first to see the risen Jesus. He could speak, and they were able to take hold of his feet in reverence.

The twelve disciples have not been seen since they all deserted Jesus and fled from Gethsemane, except for Peter, who denied him, and Judas Iscariot, who betrayed him, then killed himself. Yet Jesus now calls them 'brothers'. God has forgiven; the alienation has been healed from God's side, and the disciples may know they still belong to the family of believers. These two Marys thus become not only the first witnesses to the resurrection and the first evangelists, but also the agents of reconciliation.

Is there someone you need to be reconciled to?
Perhaps you could initiate that today.

TIM HEATON

Let me go

Jesus said to [Mary Magdalene], 'Woman, why are you weeping? For whom are you looking?' Supposing him to be the gardener, she said to him, 'Sir, if you have carried him away, tell me where you have laid him, and I will take him away.' Jesus said to her, 'Mary!' She turned and said to him in Hebrew, 'Rabbouni!' (which means Teacher). Jesus said to her, 'Do not hold on to me, because I have not yet ascended to the Father. But go to my brothers and say to them, "I am ascending to my Father and your Father, to my God and your God."'

Titian's painting 'Noli me tangere' (c. 1514) hangs in London's National Gallery. The words of the title, translated 'Do not touch me', are from the Vulgate, the Latin version of the Bible in use at the time. The King James Bible renders the same phrase 'Touch me not', while more modern versions translate the original Greek as 'Do not hold on to me.' The painting shows Mary Magdalene kneeling on the ground with one hand outstretched towards Jesus as he appears to sidestep her.

'Do not hold on to me': Jesus' glorification – his crucifixion, resurrection and ascension – is not yet complete; nothing must interfere with the unfolding of these events. Accordingly, Jesus' words are not a prohibition against touching his resurrected body (others will soon be invited to do just that) but an injunction against frustrating his imminent ascension and return to God. The desire to hold on to the bodily form of the risen Jesus must be resisted, so as not to impede the bestowal of the Holy Spirit and a new abiding relationship with God. The good news that Jesus commands Mary to proclaim is not that he is risen but that he is ascending.

Don't tell Titian, but I find his painting rather unsatisfying. It's beautifully painted, of course, but I'd always imagined Mary throwing her arms around Jesus in an enormous bear hug, the kind of embrace that says, 'I'm never going to let you go!' Because isn't that what you'd do?

Jesus has promised to 'prepare a place for you' (John 14:2).
His ascension ensures the fulfilment of that promise to those he loves.

TIM HEATON

Companion on the road

Now on that same day two of them were going to a village called Emmaus, about seven miles from Jerusalem, and talking with each other about all these things that had happened. While they were talking and discussing, Jesus himself came near and went with them, but their eyes were kept from recognising him. And he said to them, 'What are you discussing with each other while you walk along?' They stood still, looking sad.

On his second Antarctic expedition, in 1914, Sir Ernest Shackleton and his team of explorers became stranded in the polar wilderness. Their ship *Endurance*, beset by sea ice before even reaching Antarctica, was crushed and sank. Shackleton and his men faced a perilous journey over hundreds of miles to safety. Remarkably, all of them survived. More remarkably still, at the extremity of their strength, on the bleakest and most hopeless part of the journey, they had the constant delusion that there was one more person with them than could actually be counted.

In the afternoon of the first Easter, Cleopas and another disciple are walking together to Emmaus, perhaps returning home after having travelled to Jerusalem for Passover. They're trying to piece together what has happened, mulling over Jesus' betrayal, arrest, trial and crucifixion, and finally the strange tale of the women at the tomb. They are downcast and gloomy and they have been slow, like everyone else, to grasp the message about the Messiah. Then Jesus himself comes alongside them.

It is not the persuasive power of the empty tomb that leads to faith but a personal encounter with the risen Jesus. Resurrection faith does not depend upon a rolling stone, the word of angels or some neatly folded grave clothes. Resurrection faith is grounded in lived experience, in the presence of Christ in everyday human existence. The risen Lord meets us on the road to our Emmauses, in the ordinary times and places of our being, and when he does, life will never be the same again.

'You'll never walk alone', as Rodgers and Hammerstein wrote in Carousel. *This is true, because God is always with us, but we must still be open to his presence and alert for the stranger who comes near and walks with us.*

TIM HEATON

The peacemaker

When it was evening on that day, the first day of the week, and the doors of the house where the disciples had met were locked for fear of the Jews, Jesus came and stood among them and said, 'Peace be with you.' After he said this, he showed them his hands and his side. Then the disciples rejoiced when they saw the Lord.

When I was in the army I served as a peacekeeper in Northern Ireland. Our job was to support the Royal Ulster Constabulary in quelling the violence between unionists and nationalists across the sectarian divide. I was there in 1979, when Pope John Paul II visited Ireland as a 'pilgrim of peace'. He'd hoped to visit Northern Ireland as well but the security situation there rendered it impossible. I still remember his great speech in Drogheda: 'Christ is waiting for you, longing for each one of you to come to him, so that he may say to each of you: your sins are forgiven; go in peace.'

If the disciples had believed Mary Magdalene's report that morning, they might not have been so afraid of the Jewish authorities. After all, their man had been vindicated; Jesus was who he said he was all along. If they were in two minds about it, I suppose they must also have been a little worried about seeing Jesus again. Apart from John, who was at the cross, they had all abandoned him that dreadful night in the olive grove, and they must have wondered how he would react when he finally caught up with them. What would he say?

'Peace be with you.' I bet they weren't expecting that. 'Call yourselves friends?' maybe, or 'Thanks for sticking up for me!', but not the gift of his peace. The first words of the risen Jesus to the gathered disciples must have been music to their ears. You can almost feel the fear and anxiety melting away. Now they can face the future with confidence, living securely in the peace of Christ, which provides a sense of security that no locked doors can give.

'Peace I leave with you; my peace I give to you.
I do not give to you as the world gives' (John 14:27).

TIM HEATON

Flesh and bones

[Jesus] said to [the disciples], 'Why are you frightened, and why do doubts arise in your hearts? Look at my hands and my feet; see that it is I myself. Touch me and see; for a ghost does not have flesh and bones as you see that I have.' And when he had said this, he showed them his hands and his feet. While in their joy they were disbelieving and still wondering, he said to them, 'Have you anything here to eat?' They gave him a piece of broiled fish, and he took it and ate in their presence.

What do ghosts eat for supper? Spooketti. What is a ghost's favourite pudding? I scream and booberries. I could go on, but I'll spare you the pain! There is evidence that some people in New Testament times believed in ghosts and that part of the mythology surrounding apparitions was that ghosts couldn't eat.

In contrast to John's account, which we looked at yesterday, Luke's record of the first appearance of the risen Jesus to the eleven and their companions in Jerusalem includes additional convincing evidence of the reality of his physical body. As in John, Jesus shows them his wounds. He also invites them to touch him to prove he is solid flesh and not an apparition, yet they were still 'disbelieving'. So he gives them more: he eats in front of them.

What place do these 'proofs' of the resurrection have for us today? The resurrection of Jesus is not an event we can subject to rational verification; we were not there. Once again, it is the effect of the living Lord on the individual believer and on the community of believers that is the foundation of faith. The most convincing proof of the resurrection is the daily testimony of the faithful that Christ still lives and that the work of his kingdom continues. The uniqueness of the Easter message is that it changes the lives of those who are touched by it.

If you believe the Lord is risen, how has it changed your life?
What do you think he has sent you to do?

TIM HEATON

The faith giver

But Thomas (who was called the Twin), one of the twelve, was not with them when Jesus came… A week later his disciples were again in the house, and Thomas was with them. Although the doors were shut, Jesus came and stood among them and said, 'Peace be with you.' Then he said to Thomas, 'Put your finger here and see my hands. Reach out your hand and put it in my side. Do not doubt but believe.' Thomas answered him, 'My Lord and my God!'

If you've never read Stuart Jackman's book *The Davidson Affair* (1998), I'd like to recommend it. It sets the events of the first Easter in a modern-day context, with various biblical characters giving their version of events to a TV news team. In the book, Thomas tells the interviewer: 'Mary Magdala reckons she saw him this morning. Put her arms round him, so she says. Talked to him and everything. Fair enough. When that happens to me I'll believe too. But until I see him alive and touch him – make sure it's really him – I'm not falling for any stories about dead men rising.'

The story of Jesus' appearance to Thomas, which is unique to John, has for ever earned this unfortunate disciple the epithet 'Doubting Thomas'. But I think that's unfair. Thomas has, in fact, acted no differently from the other disciples, who didn't seem to believe Mary's earlier testimony either. What Thomas demanded as the conditions of his belief is no more than what Jesus had already given the others (John 20:20; Luke 24:39).

Thomas, then, is perhaps a caricature of all the disciples in their disbelief, and the centre of this story is not Thomas but Jesus. At its heart is Jesus' generous and gracious offer of himself, giving Thomas nothing less than he asked for. Jesus doesn't censure Thomas for these conditions; instead he gives him exactly what he needs for faith. His faith is more important than the grounds of his faith. It is, in the end, a story of hope and promise, not judgement and reprimand.

What Thomas saw evoked the most complete confession of faith: 'My Lord and my God!' How did you, who have not seen, come to believe that God is fully revealed in Jesus?

TIM HEATON

Pass it on

For I handed on to you as of first importance what I in turn had received: that Christ died for our sins in accordance with the scriptures, and that he was buried, and that he was raised on the third day in accordance with the scriptures, and that he appeared to Cephas, then to the twelve. Then he appeared to more than five hundred brothers and sisters at one time, most of whom are still alive, though some have died. Then he appeared to James, then to all the apostles.

The story of the resurrection is not fiction or fantasy. It reaches back to the word of eyewitnesses, those who could actually say, 'I saw him.' In the end it is their story, and over time the historical details of the events of Holy Week and Easter were told to others by those who had first-hand experience of them. Here, the apostle Paul hands on to the Corinthian church what he himself had heard, presumably from the witnesses he mentions. It's worth remembering that Paul didn't have the gospel narratives known to us, which were all written later, so this is an independent record.

The appearance to Cephas, which is the Aramaic form of Peter, is also attested by Luke 24:34. It's possible that Luke, who was a friend and missionary companion of Paul, knew about this from Paul. The appearance to 'more than five hundred' is not referred to in any other part of the New Testament. James was the brother of Jesus, and this experience might account for the fact that James, while not a disciple of Jesus during his ministry, quickly emerges as one of the leaders of the Jerusalem church. Though he was not a believer previously, his encounter with the risen Jesus immediately brought faith to life within him.

The resurrection of Jesus and his subsequent appearances to a long list of witnesses is at the very heart of the gospel proclaimed in the church. Those who saw him were changed, and what they preached centred not on the life and teachings of Jesus but on his death and resurrection. Without this foundational truth there would be no church, because there would be no gospel.

Will you tell someone the good news today?

TIM HEATON

Cast the net

Just after daybreak, Jesus stood on the beach; but the disciples did not know that it was Jesus. Jesus said to them, 'Children, you have no fish, have you?' They answered him, 'No.' He said to them, 'Cast the net to the right side of the boat, and you will find some.' So they cast it, and now they were not able to haul it in because there were so many fish... When they had gone ashore, they saw a charcoal fire there, with fish on it, and bread. Jesus said to them, 'Bring some of the fish that you have just caught.'

In 1933, on the north-west shore of the Sea of Galilee, the Franciscans built a black basalt stone church over the ruins of a fourth-century church. The original church had been erected over a large projection of limestone rock, flat on top and standing a couple of feet above the sand. It's the place where Christian tradition believes this breakfast of fish and bread occurred, and the outcrop of rock is still venerated today as Mensa Christi, the table of Christ. It is visited by many Christians seeking to rededicate themselves to their vocation.

The disciples have left Jerusalem and headed north to Galilee as Jesus had instructed them (Matthew 28:10). It seems there was time for a spot of fishing, reminding us of the original occupation of the first disciples and the place of their calling. That night they caught nothing, but Jesus' appearance to them in the morning changes everything and the fishing trip becomes symbolic of the disciples' mission. The miraculous catch of fish reminds us of their calling to become 'fishers of people', joining Jesus in his task of drawing people to God.

Our missionary work today will meet with failures and frustrations; there will be times when we 'catch nothing'. But don't despair. Remember that our task is only to 'cast the net' and do our best to cooperate with the workings of the Holy Spirit. On that alone will we be judged, not on the catch, which the Lord shall provide. God is full of surprises for those who are willing to listen and, at his command, cast the net.

'Follow me and I will make you fish for people' (Mark 1:17).

TIM HEATON

Always with you

Now the eleven disciples went to Galilee, to the mountain to which Jesus had directed them. When they saw him, they worshipped him; but some doubted. And Jesus came and said to them, 'All authority in heaven and on earth has been given to me. Go therefore and make disciples of all nations, baptising them in the name of the Father and of the Son and of the Holy Spirit, and teaching them to obey everything that I have commanded you. And remember, I am with you always, to the end of the age.'

This scene is beautifully imagined in the 2016 film *Risen*: at dawn, the day after the breakfast on the beach, Jesus commissions the eleven to make his church an inclusive community of all people, entered through baptism. He then walks away from them towards the rising sun, silhouetted against the fiery disc of light, before vanishing from their sight. As the disciples gaze on, the sun continues its ascent in the eastern sky.

I love that image: the last sighting of Jesus against the life-giving sun, the sun that danced on Easter Day. Though Matthew does not narrate the ascension as such, the time had come for Jesus to return to God and make way for the coming of the Holy Spirit. His bodily presence was no longer necessary to his followers, but he would always be spiritually present with them 'to the end of the age'. Jesus assumes his throne and begins to reign, before coming again 'on the clouds of heaven' (Matthew 24:30) at the end of history.

'But some doubted.' Does this refer to some of the eleven or to others besides the eleven? Though it may seem strange, perhaps the former is meant. Was the mind playing tricks again? The mixed response is typical of the disciples and of discipleship generally, which is always a matter of 'little faith'. The resurrection sounds so implausible and is so beyond human understanding that it seems it didn't generate absolute faith even in those who experienced it first-hand. It was not to perfect believers that the world mission was entrusted but to a wavering community of worshippers – people a bit like us.

'You of little faith, why did you doubt?' (Matthew 14:31).

TIM HEATON

This page is left blank for your notes

Reading *New Daylight* in a group

SALLY WELCH

I am aware that although some of you cherish the moments of quiet during the day which enable you to read and reflect on the passages we offer you in *New Daylight*, other readers prefer to study in small groups, to enable conversation and discussion and the sharing of insights. With this in mind, here are some ideas for discussion starters within a study group. Some of the questions are generic and can be applied to any set of contributions within this issue; others are specific to certain sets of readings. I hope that they generate some interesting reflections and conversations!

General discussion starters

These can be used for any study series within this issue. Remember there are no right or wrong answers – these questions are simply to enable a group to engage in conversation.

- What do you think the main idea or theme of the author in this series? Do you think they succeeded in communicating this to you, or were you more interested in the side issues?
- Have you had any experience of the issues that are raised in the study? How have they affected your life?
- What evidence does the author use to support their ideas? Do they use personal observations and experience, facts, quotations from other authorities? Which appeals to you most?
- Does the author make a 'call to action'? Is that call realistic and achievable? Do you think their ideas will work in the secular world?
- Can you identify specific passages that struck you personally – as interesting, profound, difficult to understand or illuminating?
- Did you learn something new reading this series? Will you think differently about some things, and if so, what are they?

Exile (Michael Mitton)

What types of exile have you experienced/are you experiencing in life? What has been particularly difficult about them? How did you manage/are you managing them? Where has God been for you in each situation?

Place (Liz Hoare)

What has surprised you about places and their significance in the life of Jesus on earth? Are there places in your life story that bring to mind something Jesus said about himself? Where are these places and what was it about them that spoke to you about the Lord?

'Enter his gates with thanksgiving, and his courts with praise' (Psalm 100).

How are you going to respond to God's loving faithfulness? Think of ways of thanksgiving and praise that might include worship but that also go beyond the boundaries of the church building, and even the church community.

Author profile: Margaret Silf

**You describe yourself as an 'ecumenical Christian'.
Can you elaborate?**

My spiritual journey has always been ecumenical. Baptised into the Methodist Church, I went to Sunday school there. I later joined a Girl Guide company that was attached to the local Anglican church and I was confirmed at the age of 15. I married a lapsed Catholic, and was received into the Roman Catholic church. I regard these three traditions as the three main roots of my spiritual life, for which I am deeply grateful.

Over the past decade I have loosened my attachment to institutional religious practice, and now I have two 'spiritual homes': the first is a small group of fellow pilgrims who meet to share journeys and support and nourish each other; the second is the local Quaker meeting, at which I am an attender. The divisions and demarcations between different Christian denominations no longer really have any meaning for me, which is why I regard myself as genuinely 'ecumenical'.

You also lead retreats. Tell us about these.

A retreat is a time and space in which people can step back temporarily from the business of daily life in order to reflect on where they are with God, either alone, in a group or with a companion. People find this deepens their relationship with God and, in doing so, nourishes their relationships with others.

Which writers have influenced your spiritual life?

The writings (and the personal friendship) of the late Gerard Hughes SJ, who connects spirituality with everyday life, are a significant influence. Also the Franciscan Richard Rohr, who takes Catholic spirituality into new realms of inter-faith, non-dualistic thinking and a more universal understanding of God. And of course, George Fox and the early Quakers touch my life regularly as we explore their writings in our local meeting.

Where will you be in five years' time?

In five years' time I may well have departed the planet. If so, I hope to be where the truth of Julian of Norwich's insight becomes clear, that 'all shall be well, and all manner of things shall be well'. Otherwise I will let God surprise me, and, as the Celts say, hope to 'dance to the music of the Spirit'.

Recommended reading

Here is an original way of approaching Lent, one that will encourage you to consider your own faith journey in the light of the Easter story. Inspired by Ian McGregor's BBC Radio 4 programme, 'The History of the World in 100 Objects', Gordon Giles spends each week in a different room gleaning spiritual lessons from everyday household objects. As a result, you might discover that finding God in the normal pattern of life – even in the mundane – transforms how you approach each day. Running as a thread through it all are the seven Rs of Lent: regret, repentance, resolution, recognition, reconciliation, renewal and resurrection.

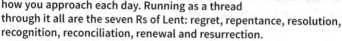

The following is taken from the introduction.

Is your home your spiritual castle? The origins of the proverb 'An Englishman's home is his castle' date back to the 16th century, when in 1581 Henri Estienne's *The Stage of Popish Toyes: conteining both tragicall and comicall partes*, stated that 'youre house is youre Castell', and in the same year Richard Mulcaster, the headmaster of the Merchant Taylor's School in London, wrote, 'He (the householder) is the appointer of his owne circumstance, and his house is his castle.' Seventy years later the lawyer and politician Sir Edward Coke established the idea in law in *The Institutes of the Laws of England* (1628): 'For a man's house is his castle, *et domus sua cuique est tutissimum refugium* [and one's home is one's safest refuge].' Another century later and none other than William Pitt the Elder said in parliament, 'The poorest man may in his cottage bid defiance to all the forces of the crown. It may be frail – its roof may shake – the wind may blow through it – the storm may enter – the rain may enter – but the King of England cannot enter.' The concept has carried across the seas to other lands too, notably to the USA, where in 1800 Joel Chandler Harris adapted the maxim, writing, 'Exalt the citizen. As the State is the unit of government he is the unit of the State. Teach him that his home is his castle, and his sovereignty rests beneath his hat.'

Notwithstanding the modern right of the police and bailiffs to force their way into premises with the necessary warrant or court order, we generally believe and behave as though our homes are private and open only to those whom we invite in. In our homes, we flee from the presence of all but our nearest and dearest. While for some it can be a place of domestic violence, treachery or strife, for many the home is a sanctuary, a safe haven and the place where not only our hearts but our belongings are housed. Increasingly, we have more and more possessions, and our homes are become warehouses for objects whose use, meaning and significance ranges widely. It is said that nature abhors a vacuum; in modern times this means that no matter how big your home is, it will likely be full of stuff!

This book, like any book, seeks to cross the threshold of the Christian home. By all means read it on the train, but its desire is to be invited in and its purpose is to snoop around and ask nosy questions about the things you have in your home. If we feel that our homes are our castles, open only to those we wish to invite in, then this book stands at the door knocking as a friend, a divine friend, even. For, as the psalmist reminds us, there is no place where we can flee from the presence of God:

> O Lord, you have searched me and known me.
> You know when I sit down and when I rise up;
> you discern my thoughts from far away.
> You search out my path and my lying down,
> and are acquainted with all my ways.
> Even before a word is on my tongue,
> O Lord, you know it completely.
> You hem me in, behind and before,
> and lay your hand upon me.
> Such knowledge is too wonderful for me;
> it is so high that I cannot attain it.
>
> Where can I go from your spirit?
> Or where can I flee from your presence?
> If I ascend to heaven, you are there;
> if I make my bed in Sheol, you are there.
> If I take the wings of the morning
> and settle at the farthest limits of the sea,
> even there your hand shall lead me,
> and your right hand shall hold me fast.
> If I say, 'Surely the darkness shall cover me,
> and the light around me become night,'
> even the darkness is not dark to you;

the night is as bright as the day,
for darkness is as light to you.
PSALM 139:1–12

Against the temptation to hide or flee from the Lord, this book of daily readings comes as an invitation to discover how he is already in our homes and as a map of where to seek and find God in the fixtures, fittings and phenomena with which we surround ourselves at home. Inspired by Ian McGregor's 2010 BBC Radio 4 series 'The History of the World in 100 Objects', this book seeks to open access to the spiritual significance of 46 objects that can be found in almost any home. Our biblical ancestors did not have anything like as much 'stuff' as we do, but some of the things we possess have long histories, while other modern gadgets and household paraphernalia have something to say to us about the world in which we live and move and have our being, and the God from whom all art and science comes. For the way we live is a spiritual as well as practical matter, and under God it is good to reflect on the things we take so much for granted.

The Holy Spirit of God is everywhere and in everything, if only we look with the right eyes and a humble frame of mind. During Lent, we are called to read and reflect, to be penitent and patient, and to journey towards the renewing light of the Easter dawn. When Easter comes in seven weeks it is my hope and prayer for you, gentle reader, that the journey around your home will cast Passiontide and Easter in a different hue, and that the Lord will have been with you in everything, and everywhere.

To order a copy of this book, please use the order form on page 149.

This inspirational book takes the reader through the 40 days of Lent to the celebration of Easter through the eyes and beliefs of Celtic Christianity. Drawing on primary sources of pastoral letters, monastic rules and the theological teaching of the Celtic church, the author presents a different perspective on the cross of Christ and draws us to see our own life journeys with a new and transforming vision.

Celtic Lent
40 days of devotion to Easter
David Cole
pb, 978 0 85746 637 2 £8.99
brfonline.org.uk

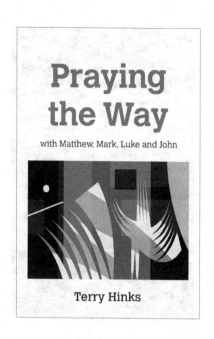

Through raw and authentic prayers, based on the gospel stories, Terry Hinks leads readers into the heart of the gospels the more clearly to see the needs and joys of today's world. This highly original book helps readers to pray out of, and with, the words of Jesus and to discover the joy of prayer as a two-way conversation – listening as much as speaking to God.

Praying the Way
With Matthew, Mark, Luke and John
Terry Hinks
pb, 978 0 85746 716 4 £10.99
brfonline.org.uk

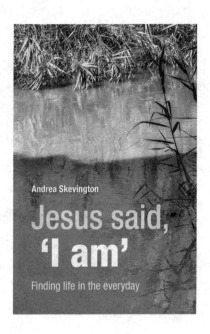

Drawing on the imagery of the Hebrew scriptures, Jesus identifies himself as the 'I am' of Israel's narrative. Through sensitive retelling, thoughtful discussion and creative exercises, Andrea Skevington shows the transforming power of Jesus' words. *Jesus Said, 'I Am'* integrates faith and imagination, story and study, helping the reader towards a well-grounded and more profound faith.

Jesus Said, 'I Am'
Finding life in the everyday
Andrea Skevington
pb 978 0 85746 562 7 £8.99
brfonline.org.uk

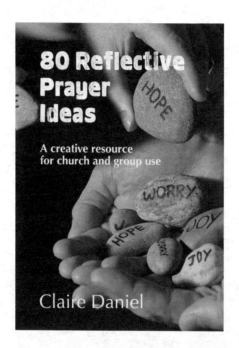

Prayer remains a vital part of Christian discipleship. Following the success of the author's *80 Creative Prayer Ideas*, this ready-to-use resource book contains 80 further ideas on setting up reflective and creative prayer stations or responses. Claire Daniel shows us how to pray with our whole being – our senses as well as our voice, our hearts as much as our minds. Tried and tested, these ideas will enhance the praying of small groups, churches and individuals.

80 Reflective Prayer Ideas
A creative resource for church and group use
Claire Daniel
pb, 978 0 85746 673 0 £12.99
brfonline.org.uk

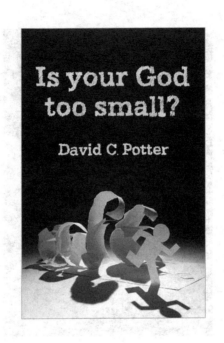

Job struggled, as we do, with huge questions – his own and the world's. He and his friends looked for an answer in the past, but discovered that the answer lay elsewhere – in God himself, and in the divine presence in his life. In an accessible way, David Potter opens up fresh insight into the book of Job, with a different perspective on our sufferings and perhaps on God.

Is Your God Too Small?
Enlarging our vision in the face of life's struggles
David C. Potter
pb, 978 0 85746 633 4 £8.99
brfonline.org.uk

Delivery times within the UK are normally 15 working days. Prices are correct at the time of going to press but may change without prior notice.

itle	Price	Qty	Total
eally Useful Guides: Psalms	£6.99		
eally Useful Guides: Colossians and Philemon	£5.99		
⋅t Home in Lent	£8.99		
⋅eltic Lent	£8.99		
⋅raying the Way	£10.99		
⋅esus Said, 'I Am'	£8.99		
⋅0 Reflective Prayer Ideas	£12.99		
⋅ Your God Too Small?	£8.99		

POSTAGE AND PACKING CHARGES			
⋅der value	UK	Europe	Rest of world
⋅der £7.00	£2.00	£5.00	£7.00
⋅00–£29.99	£3.00	£9.00	£15.00
⋅0.00 and over	FREE	£9.00 + 15% of order value	£15.00 + 20% of order value

Total value of books	
Postage and packing	
Total for this order	

⋅ase complete in **BLOCK CAPITALS**

itle .... First name/initials .... Surname.................................

⋅ddress ....

.... Postcode ....

⋅cc. No. .... Telephone ....

⋅mail ....

⋅ethod of payment

❏ Cheque (made payable to BRF)   ❏ MasterCard / Visa

⋅ard no. ☐☐☐☐ ☐☐☐☐ ☐☐☐☐ ☐☐☐☐

⋅alid from ☐M☐M ☐Y☐Y   Expires ☐M☐M ☐Y☐Y   Security code* ☐☐☐

Last 3 digits on the reverse of the card

⋅ignature* .... Date ..../........../..........

⋅SSENTIAL IN ORDER TO PROCESS YOUR ORDER

⋅ase return this form to: BRF, 15 The Chambers, Vineyard, Abingdon OX14 3FE | enquiries@brf.org.uk

⋅ead our terms and find out about cancelling your order, please visit **brfonline.org.uk/terms**.

The Bible Reading Fellowship (BRF) is a Registered Charity (233280)

How to encourage Bible reading in your church

BRF has been helping individuals connect with the Bible for over 90 years. We want to support churches as they seek to encourage church members into regular Bible reading.

Order a Bible reading resources pack

This pack is designed to give your church the tools to publicise our Bible reading notes. It includes:

- Sample Bible reading notes for your congregation to try.
- Publicity resources, including a poster.
- A church magazine feature about Bible reading notes.

The pack is free, but we welcome a £5 donation to cover the cost of postage. If you require a pack to be sent outside the UK or require a specific number of sample Bible reading notes, please contact us for postage costs. More information about what the current pack contains is available on our website.

How to order and find out more

- Visit **biblereadingnotes.org.uk/for-churches**
- Telephone BRF on +44 (0)1865 319700 Mon–Fri 9.15–17.30
- Write to us at BRF, 15 The Chambers, Vineyard, Abingdon OX14 3FE

Keep informed about our latest initiatives

We are continuing to develop resources to help churches encourage people into regular Bible reading, wherever they are on their journey. Join our email list at **biblereadingnotes.org.uk/helpingchurches** to stay informed about the latest initiatives that your church could benefit from.

Introduce a friend to our notes

We can send information about our notes and current prices for you to pass on. Please contact us.

Transforming lives and communities

BRF is a charity that is passionate about making a difference through the Christian faith. We want to see lives and communities transformed through our creative programmes and resources for individuals, churches and schools. We are doing this by resourcing:

- **Christian growth and understanding of the Bible.** Through our Bible reading notes, books, digital resources, conferences and other events, we're resourcing individuals, groups and leaders in churches for their own spiritual journey and for their ministry.
- **Church outreach in the local community.** BRF is the home of Messy Church and The Gift of Years, programmes that churches are embracing to great effect as they seek to engage with their communities.
- **Teaching Christianity in primary schools.** Our Barnabas in Schools team is working with primary-aged children and their teachers, enabling them to explore Christianity creatively and confidently within the school curriculum.
- **Children's and family ministry.** Through our Parenting for Faith programme, websites and published resources, we're working with churches and families, enabling children and adults alike to explore Christianity creatively and bring the Bible alive.

Do you share our vision?

Sales of our books and Bible reading notes cover the cost of producing them. However, our other programmes are funded primarily by donations, grants and legacies. If you share our vision, would you help us to transform even more lives and communities? Your prayers and financial support are vital for the work that we do. You could:

- support BRF's ministry with a regular donation (at **brf.org.uk/donate**);
- support us with a one-off gift (use the form on pages 153–54);
- consider leaving a gift to BRF in your will (see page 152);
- encourage your church to support BRF as part of your church's giving to home mission – perhaps focusing on a specific area of our ministry, or a particular member of our Barnabas in Schools team.
- most important of all, support BRF with your prayers.

Giving for the future

The feast day of St Finan is celebrated on 17 February. Now largely lost within the Anglican tradition, feast days are an annual celebration of a saint, usually marked by prayers and a relevant Bible reading.

Finan lived during the seventh century AD and became bishop of Lindisfarne when Aidan, the founder of the now-famous monastery, died. In his book, *40 Days with the Celtic Saints: Devotional readings for a time of preparation*, David Cole writes:

> Finan's heart for mission, as well as his tenacity in his belief, marked him out as a great man of faith and inner strength. His influence spread throughout England...

In 2004, a church near Portsmouth with a 'heart for mission' stepped out into the unknown and launched the first Messy Church. They had no idea that 15 years later its influence would spread not only throughout England but also around the world. Today, there are almost 4,000 Messy Churches in over 25 countries.

BRF is the home of Messy Church and through it we are helping families become followers of Jesus. For almost a century we have been able to fund the growth, development and sustainability of programmes, like Messy Church, thanks to the generosity of those who support us through gifts in wills.

If you share our vision for transforming lives through the Christian faith, would you consider leaving a gift in your will to BRF? It doesn't need to be huge to help us make a real difference.

For further information about making a gift to BRF in your will, please visit **brf.org.uk/lastingdifference**, contact Sophie Aldred on **+44 (0)1865 319700** or email **giving@brf.org.uk**.

Whatever you can do or give, we thank you for your support.

SHARING OUR VISION – MAKING A GIFT

I would like to make a gift to support BRF. Please use my gift for:

☐ where it is needed most ☐ Barnabas in Schools ☐ Parenting for Faith
☐ Messy Church ☐ The Gift of Years

Title	First name/initials	Surname

Address

	Postcode

Email

Telephone

Signature	Date

gift aid it You can add an extra 25p to every £1 you give.

Please treat as Gift Aid donations all qualifying gifts of money made

☐ today, ☐ in the past four years, ☐ and in the future.

I am a UK taxpayer and understand that if I pay less Income Tax and/or Capital Gains Tax in the current tax year than the amount of Gift Aid claimed on all my donations, it is my responsibility to pay any difference.

☐ My donation does not qualify for Gift Aid.

Please notify BRF if you want to cancel this Gift Aid declaration, change your name or home address, or no longer pay sufficient tax on your income and/or capital gains.

Please complete other side of form ➜

Please return this form to:
BRF, 15 The Chambers, Vineyard, Abingdon OX14 3FE

The Bible Reading Fellowship is a Registered Charity (233280)

SHARING OUR VISION – MAKING A GIFT

Regular giving

By Direct Debit: You can set up a Direct Debit quickly and easily at **brf.org.uk/donate**

By Standing Order: Please contact our Fundraising Administrator
+44 (0)1235 462305 | giving@brf.org.uk

One-off donation

Please accept my gift of:

☐ £10 ☐ £50 ☐ £100 Other £ _____

by (delete as appropriate):

☐ Cheque/Charity Voucher payable to 'BRF'

☐ MasterCard/Visa/Debit card/Charity card

Name on card

Card no. ☐☐☐☐ ☐☐☐☐ ☐☐☐☐ ☐☐☐☐

Valid from M M Y Y   Expires M M Y Y

Security code* ☐☐☐ *Last 3 digits on the reverse of the card
ESSENTIAL IN ORDER TO PROCESS YOUR PAYMENT

Signature | Date

☐ I would like to leave a gift in my will to BRF.

For more information, visit **brf.org.uk/lastingdifference**

For help or advice regarding making a gift, please contact our Fundraising Administrator +44 (0)1235 462305

➤ Please complete other side of form

Please return this form to:
BRF, 15 The Chambers, Vineyard, Abingdon OX14 3FE

The Bible Reading Fellowship is a Registered Charity (233280)

ND0119

NEW DAYLIGHT SUBSCRIPTION RATES

Please note our new subscription rates, current until 30 April 2020:

Individual subscriptions
covering 3 issues for under 5 copies, payable in advance
(including postage & packing):

	UK	Europe	Rest of world
New Daylight	£17.40	£25.50	£29.40
New Daylight 3-year subscription (9 issues) (not available for Deluxe)	£49.50	N/A	N/A
New Daylight Deluxe per set of 3 issues p.a.	£21.90	£32.40	£38.40

Group subscriptions
covering 3 issues for 5 copies or more, sent to **one** UK address (post free):

New Daylight	£13.80 per set of 3 issues p.a.
New Daylight Deluxe	£17.55 per set of 3 issues p.a.

Please note that the annual billing period for group subscriptions runs from 1 May to 30 April.

Overseas group subscription rates
Available on request. Please email **enquiries@brf.org.uk**.

Copies may also be obtained from Christian bookshops:

New Daylight	£4.60 per copy
New Daylight Deluxe	£5.85 per copy

All our Bible reading notes can be ordered online by visiting
biblereadingnotes.org.uk/subscriptions

For information about our other Bible reading notes,
and apps for iPhone and iPod touch, visit
biblereadingnotes.org.uk

NEW DAYLIGHT INDIVIDUAL SUBSCRIPTION FORM

All our Bible reading notes can be ordered online by visiting
biblereadingnotes.org.uk/subscriptions

☐ I would like to take out a subscription:

Title .... First name/initials .... Surname ....

Address ....

.... Postcode ....

Telephone .... Email ....

Please send *New Daylight* beginning with the May 2019 / September 2019 / January 2020 issue
(*delete as appropriate*):

(*please tick box*)

	UK	Europe	Rest of world
New Daylight 1-year subscription	☐ £17.40	☐ £25.50	☐ £29.40
New Daylight 3-year subscription	☐ £49.50	N/A	N/A
New Daylight Deluxe	☐ £21.90	☐ £32.40	☐ £38.40

Total enclosed £ .... (cheques should be made payable to 'BRF')

Please charge my MasterCard / Visa ☐ Debit card ☐ with £ ....

Card no. ☐☐☐☐ ☐☐☐☐ ☐☐☐☐ ☐☐☐☐

Valid from ☐☐☐☐ Expires ☐☐☐☐ Security code* ☐☐☐

Last 3 digits on the reverse of the card

Signature* .... Date ....../....../......

*ESSENTIAL IN ORDER TO PROCESS YOUR PAYMENT

To set up a Direct Debit, please also complete the Direct Debit instruction on page 159
and return it to BRF with this form.

Please return this form with the appropriate payment to:
BRF, 15 The Chambers, Vineyard, Abingdon OX14 3FE

To read our terms and find out about cancelling your order, please visit **brfonline.org.uk/terms**.

The Bible Reading Fellowship is a Registered Charity (233280)

ND0119

NEW DAYLIGHT GIFT SUBSCRIPTION FORM

☐ I would like to give a gift subscription (please provide both names and addresses):

Title .... First name/initials .... Surname ....

Address ....

.... Postcode ....

Telephone .... Email ....

Gift subscription name ....

Gift subscription address ....

.... Postcode ....

Gift message (20 words max. or include your own gift card):

....

....

Please send *New Daylight* beginning with the May 2019 / September 2019 / January 2020 issue (*delete as appropriate*):

(*please tick box*)

	UK	Europe	Rest of world
New Daylight 1-year subscription	☐ £17.40	☐ £25.50	☐ £29.40
New Daylight 3-year subscription	☐ £49.50	N/A	N/A
New Daylight Deluxe	☐ £21.90	☐ £32.40	☐ £38.40

Total enclosed £ .... (cheques should be made payable to 'BRF')

Please charge my MasterCard / Visa ☐ Debit card ☐ with £ ....

Card no. ☐☐☐☐ ☐☐☐☐ ☐☐☐☐ ☐☐☐☐

Valid from ☐☐/☐☐   Expires ☐☐/☐☐   Security code* ☐☐☐

Last 3 digits on the reverse of the card

Signature* .... Date ....../....../......

*ESSENTIAL IN ORDER TO PROCESS YOUR PAYMENT

To set up a Direct Debit, please also complete the Direct Debit instruction on page 159 and return it to BRF with this form.

Please return this form with the appropriate payment to:
BRF, 15 The Chambers, Vineyard, Abingdon OX14 3FE

To read our terms and find out about cancelling your order, please visit **brfonline.org.uk/terms**.

The Bible Reading Fellowship is a Registered Charity (233280)

DIRECT DEBIT PAYMENT

You can pay for your annual subscription to our Bible reading notes using Direct Debit. You need only give your bank details once, and the payment is made automatically every year until you cancel it. If you would like to pay by Direct Debit, please use the form opposite, entering your BRF account number under 'Reference number'.

You are fully covered by the Direct Debit Guarantee:

The Direct Debit Guarantee

- This Guarantee is offered by all banks and building societies that accept instructions to pay Direct Debits.
- If there are any changes to the amount, date or frequency of your Direct Debit, The Bible Reading Fellowship will notify you 10 working days in advance of your account being debited or as otherwise agreed. If you request The Bible Reading Fellowship to collect a payment, confirmation of the amount and date will be given to you at the time of the request.
- If an error is made in the payment of your Direct Debit, by The Bible Reading Fellowship or your bank or building society, you are entitled to a full and immediate refund of the amount paid from your bank or building society.
- If you receive a refund you are not entitled to, you must pay it back when The Bible Reading Fellowship asks you to.
- You can cancel a Direct Debit at any time by simply contacting your bank or building society. Written confirmation may be required. Please also notify us.

The Bible Reading Fellowship

Instruction to your bank or building society to pay by Direct Debit

Please fill in the whole form using a ballpoint pen and return it to:
BRF, 15 The Chambers, Vineyard, Abingdon OX14 3FE

Service User Number: | 5 | 5 | 8 | 2 | 2 | 9 |

Name and full postal address of your bank or building society

To: The Manager	Bank/Building Society
Address	
	Postcode

Name(s) of account holder(s)

Branch sort code

| | | | – | | | | – | | | |

Bank/Building Society account number

| | | | | | | | | | |

Reference number

| | | | | | | | |

Instruction to your Bank/Building Society
Please pay The Bible Reading Fellowship Direct Debits from the account detailed in this instruction, subject to the safeguards assured by the Direct Debit Guarantee. I understand that this instruction may remain with The Bible Reading Fellowship and, if so, details will be passed electronically to my bank/building society.

Signature(s)

Banks and Building Societies may not accept Direct Debit instructions for some types of account.

BRF

Transforming
lives and communities

Christian growth and understanding of the Bible

Resourcing individuals, groups and leaders in churches for their own spiritual journey and for their ministry

Church outreach in the local community

Offering two programmes that churches are embracing to great effect as they seek to engage with their local communities and transform lives

Teaching Christianity in primary schools

Working with children and teachers to explore Christianity creatively and confidently

Children's and family ministry

Working with churches and families to explore Christianity creatively and bring the Bible alive

parenting for faith

Visit **brf.org.uk** for more information on BRF's work

brf.org.uk